Vernon Higham was ....
edd, Wales. He was ....
theological college at A............... and served, in his
early ministry, Welsh-speaking churches at
Pontardulais and Llanddewi Brefi. There followed a
call in 1962 to the Heath Evangelical Church in
Cardiff, Wales, where he has continued as Pastor to
the present day. His ministry has been characterised
throughout by faithful expository Biblical preaching
– emphasising salvation by grace alone which results
in gracious, holy living – and a burden for true
revival.

Mr. Higham is the author of several Christian
books and has also written many inspiring Christian
hymns.

GOD'S WORKMANSHIP

Vernon Higham

Christian Focus

© 1997 Vernon Higham
ISBN 1 85792 255 7
Published in
1997 by
Christian Focus Publications, Geanies House, Fearn,
Ross-shire,
IV20 1TW, Great Britain.

Cover design by Donna Macleod

Contents

'Not of works, lest any man should boast. For we are His workmanship, created in Christ Jesus unto good works, which God hath before ordained that we should walk in them' (Ephesians 2:9,10).

'Wherefore, my beloved, ... work out your own salvation with fear and trembling. For it is God which worketh in you both to will and to do of His good pleasure' (Philippians 2:12,13).

PREFACE

The greatest possible experience for any person is that which brings them into a living relationship with God through the Lord Jesus Christ. This experience involves His work in saving their souls. Therefore, such value the Lord Jesus' death, which was how He bore their punishment and so freed them from the dreadful consequences of their sin. They also value His life – that wonderful life that so pleased God – for it was His fulfilling the law on their behalf which has resulted in His life of obedience being counted as theirs. This experience, and this alone, makes people Christian.

In this little book I set out to describe the adventure of grace – of a life living with God – both in its initial vital relationship and in its sure fellowship throughout the rest of our lives. It is a partnership with a very senior Partner. I am always thrilled with what Paul wrote to the Philippians: 'Work out your own salvation with fear and trembling. For it is God that worketh in you both to will and to do of His good pleasure' (Philippians 2:12-13). The implications of our salvation demand that we think things through and work things out according to spiritual principles. But we are also to understand that God works with enabling grace both in our wills and in our abilities to perform.

As God works out His wonderful plan in us, we are

also totally involved. In such a relationship there is a
sensitive awareness of that which is well pleasing in
His sight, and also of that which grieves the Holy
Spirit. In this partnership everything in our lives is
influenced – our joys and sorrows, our hopes and
fears – because we know that in all of these things we
are not alone. Even in death's dark vale, Christ is in
us, the hope of glory.

I am particularly interested in us – the Lord's
children – being unmistakably godly in the eyes of
all. This means that our very minds and affections
and decisions have a place for the Lord, that He is on
the throne of our hearts. In this new life of grace we
are to be consciously aware of God, not only thinking
about us, but working in us and refining us in such a
tender way that with heart and soul we rejoice in this
partnership. Once we are Christians we are never
alone again and we should both *know* and *feel* this.

Sometimes we might feel daunted at the expecta-
tion of God in a believer's life. But because God is
both on our side and with us we are given grace to
overcome and grace to achieve our glorious desired
end. This is life with God, the God who will not fail
or disown us but will prepare us for that day when we
shall be enjoying fellowship eternally with Him in
heaven. On our part, it calls for cooperation and
submission to His will and for us to delight in His
presence and ask for grace to love Him all the days of
our lives.

1

Regeneration

'A time to be born...'
(Ecclesiastes 3:2)

In attempting to describe the work of God's grace that results in a person becoming a Christian, it is almost impossible to know where to begin. It is like a landscape artist taking his canvas, paints and other materials, finding a vantage point in the Grand Canyon, and then wondering where he could begin his efforts to catch such breathtaking beauty. The myriad colours and shades are ever changing and ever moving as the light varies from dawn to dusk, and as the clouds overhead give way to a clear sky or even a haze of great heat. How can it be possible to convey on canvas the living canvas before his eyes? As well as that however, he would observe the strange shapes of the rocks, some rising like cathedral towers from the depths of the canyon; he would see the tempestuous Colorado river making its angry way through the valley, although seeming like a silver thread when viewed from the heights. The canvas appears so minute in the face of such grandeur, yet paint he must.

The work of grace in the human soul, however, is

far more challenging when we pause to consider the love of God and endeavour to encompass something of its depth and height and breadth. The detailed, tender touches of God's mercy in our lives leave us standing in amazement and exclaiming, with the hymnist, 'How great Thou art!'

It would be impossible to describe every person's experience and relate in detail their individual spiritual pilgrimage. Nevertheless certain essential features will be recognisable in all who are brought from death to life. There are many ways of expressing this spiritual transformation and it is necessary that we should be clear about it. There is a vast difference between being short-sighted and never having seen at all because of total blindness, or between being hard of hearing and never having heard at all. To the totally deaf, the concept of sound is as impossible to convey as colour would be to the blind. Likewise there is a vast difference between being quite unwell and being dead, and never to have had experience of life. Spiritual death means a complete eclipse of all things spiritual. Even though religious activity and knowledge are quite possible, it is something entirely different to be alive towards God.

In Ephesians 2:4-5 Paul refers to the dead being 'quickened', that is, being made alive: 'But God, who is rich in mercy, for his great love wherewith he loved us, even when we were dead in sins, hath quickened us together with Christ (by grace ye are saved).' In the first verse of the same chapter there is a similar description of being 'dead in trespasses and sins'.

Spiritual death is being 'dead in sins'.

This condition is something that everyone inherits from the first man, Adam. We call it *original sin* and it remains in our nature as a powerful principle, so that even our better activities are tainted by its influence. It is something that we cannot shake off, try as we may, neither can we gradually wean ourselves away from it. It holds us in a vice-like grip, and we are trapped and quite incapable of understanding spiritual matters. There may be much that we can do in this condition. We are able to be kind and moral, just as we are able to be the opposite. But because we are in a state of spiritual death, we cannot make a clean break or even see the necessity of doing so. Paul describes precisely the outlook of those who are spiritually dead: 'But the natural man receiveth not the things of the Spirit of God; for they are foolishness unto him: neither can he know them, because they are spiritually discerned' (1 Corinthians 2:14).

This obviously poses a problem. How can we become spiritually alive so that we are able to understand and embrace the Christian faith? The simple answer is that it is an act of God. But having said that, it does not mean that we are not involved. Never in our lives hitherto have we been involved in anything so vital.

It is only with hindsight that we can trace the beginning of things insofar as our own experience is concerned. In our view it seems to have such small beginnings.

Sometimes it is the influence of another person

who seems to have great peace, despite often having difficult and sad events in their life. We say to ourselves that, in their position, we would be over-whelmed and unable to cope. Although this person might explain the secret of their calm and how the Lord Jesus Christ has changed their total outlook, it may not make too deep or lasting an impression on us at first.

At other times we may be personally involved in circumstances that we would not have wished for ourselves, but strangely we begin to think about God and to sense a longing for something that we are not able to name. It is as if we are searching for some kind of spiritual lost chord which, if only we could find it, would put us in tune with God.

On occasions, we are invited to a Christian meet-ing and possibly we go along just to please a friend, yet we feel rather glad that we were invited and that we agreed to go.

Increasingly we become aware that something is happening to us even though, if we were challenged concerning our standing with God, we would protest and elaborate on our virtues, or grasp at any straw we could lay our hands on. We might point out we attended Sunday School as children or that our par-ents were very good people, as we desperately seek to justify ourselves. Yet hope has been born.

At this stage, there are times when we may feel overwhelmed with fear and by a sense of unworthi-ness, while at other times our hearts are thrilled by the thought of the Lord's presence. We can also be distracted very easily and for a while we may withdraw. But when God begins a work in a person's soul He never gives up, but will fulfil what He has in view for them – and that is their eternal good.

> When once Thou visitest the heart,
> Then truth begins to shine;
> Then earthly vanities depart,
> Then kindles love divine. *Edward Caswall*

There comes a time when the message of the gospel shines clearly in our souls and our involvement with the things of God becomes deeper. The mind understands and accepts that the Lord Jesus Christ is the Son of God. We are able to say 'Amen' to the answer which Peter gave our Lord when He enquired of the disciples whom He was: 'Thou art the Christ, the Son of the living God' (Matthew 16:16). What a wonderful statement! We feel it so clearly expresses what we have discovered.

However, a louder 'Amen' comes from our hearts as we grasp what the Lord Jesus meant when He replied: 'Flesh and blood hath not revealed it unto thee, but My Father which is in heaven' (Matthew 16:17). The secret activity of God's grace in revealing these things becomes clearer and clearer. The enlightened mind understands the value and spiritual implication of the life of Christ. He fulfilled God's holy law perfectly in every detail, and He did this for us. Then His Cross rises before our eyes and we see at last that this was no ordinary crucifixion. It was a penalty paid for our sins, the penalty was death. He

died in our place so that our souls would not be
condemned in the final day of Judgment. The knowledge, that our Lord lived for us a life that we could
never have lived, and died a death that we would be
forever dying, is precious. But not only does our mind
understand these things, our affections too are stirred
by such love, by such mercy and grace. From that
moment we are in our first love.

Our souls are challenged and inspired to respond.
'What shall I do?' cries out my will. 'I shall never be
good enough to be a candidate for such love.' The
will confesses many foolish decisions and actions but
feels it dares not approach the Saviour. Yet the soul
is increasingly aware of an invitation to come to
Christ, and does so with a grace that we know is
impossible to merit. Then we remember the words of
Scripture that Jesus came to seek and save those who
were lost. It is astonishing how the Holy Spirit takes
a particular verse of Scripture or a spiritual truth and
applies it to our understanding, but the end result is
that the sinner is invited to receive forgiveness. Our
will is swept along by the pardoning grace of God and
our soul whispers with quietness and humility, yet
helped by a new confidence, that it is coming to the
Saviour just as it is.

> Come, ye weary, heavy-laden,
> Bruised and broken by the fall;
> If you tarry till you're better,
> You will never come at all:
> Not the righteous –
> Sinners Jesus came to call!   *Joseph Hart*

In the approach of the soul to God, two vital features become evident. They are part of that path that all sinners tread as the enlightened mind is exercised, as the affections are stirred by holy desires and as the will has an urgency to come to Christ. I am not suggesting that all examples of conversion are mere replicas of one another; there will be a variety of influences upon us, and our characters and responses can be so different. Nevertheless there are common threads, and the two key factors are *repentance* and *faith*. These must be present if sinners are to avail themselves of the benefits of the Saviour's sinless life and His atoning death on Calvary.

It is necessary for us to be clear on the sequence in the experience of grace. Repentance towards God is sure to be an integral part of the process. There must be an element of faith in repentance in order to understand why we are repenting and feeling sorrow for our sin. It is not a superficial matter, since repentance involves us totally. The mind knows and acknowledges the fact of sin and that we are sinners who have offended against a holy God. Our affections are deeply influenced in that we have what the Bible describes as a 'godly sorrow' and a desire to change. The will is moved into positive action by this reality of sorrow for sin and this sincere desire to change: 'For godly sorrow worketh repentance to salvation not to be repented of: but the sorrow of the world worketh death' (2 Corinthians 7:10).

Faith then enters the scene as it is brought into action by the preaching of the Word of God. Here

again the mind realises the truth of the gospel and
exercises faith. We are confronted with the truth, so
that there is an element of *knowledge* in faith, otherwise it would be folly to trust something of which we
are totally ignorant. It is as if the soul gave a thoughtful look and carefully surveyed the gospel, then,
understanding and believing in its integrity, it trusts
this glorious truth.

A simple example can be used to illustrate the
difference between faith and folly. Imagine a person
who is ill being presented with a bottle of medicine
but not given any idea of its contents. The patient
drinks the medicine with disastrous results. On the
other hand, imagine a reputable doctor examining
that patient, correctly diagnosing his illness and
prescribing a bottle of medicine. The patient eagerly
accepts the bottle, fully aware of its medicinal value,
then promptly locks it in a cupboard and hides the
key. He proceeds to boast about the qualifications of
the doctor, his perfect remedy and his gratitude in
having safely in his possession the required treat-
ment. However, the patient dies, simply because he
does not partake of the medicine provided. Knowledge is valuable, but trust is equally necessary. In
partaking of the reliable remedy the patient would
have required trust in its effectiveness.

Similarly, a certain amount of knowledge of the
gospel is essential before taking that step of trusting
the Saviour with our souls. This is the function of
faith and without it we will not see God. But where
can we find such faith? 'For by grace are ye saved

through faith; and that not of yourselves: it is the gift of God' (Ephesians 2:8).

Our affections and wills are surely included because when the grace of God is at work, and our souls are responding, it is impossible to bypass our feelings and choices. We are deeply moved as the thought of the Saviour sacrificing Himself for us floods our hearts with gratitude. Then when faith is thoroughly furnished, there comes that moment of committal and, knowing the gospel and trusting the Saviour, our wills decide on that final step of faith.

There can be no greater experience in a person's life than that of becoming a Christian. Exactly as the Grand Canyon displays to our sight a multitude of colours and shapes, so Christian experience grants us glimpses of the sublime grace of God and an assurance that He is involved with His people. In a world full of uncertainty and insecurity, and in an existence that is so precarious, we find a stability, meaning and purpose that we never thought were possible. From now onwards the governing principle in our lives becomes the grace of God. Our great aim is 'to glorify God and enjoy Him forever'. It is impossible to be indifferent to such a gospel and so gracious a God.

Discovering the involvement of God

Before long we will be aware that this revelation we have received is *special*. At first we feel sure that if we explain the gospel to our friends they will understand immediately. But somehow they don't. We cannot help but be troubled at this, especially since the issue is vital to their eternal destiny. Gradually we begin to realise that there is another factor involved, and that is the activity of God. Words which are often quoted and loved, and rightly so, state, 'And him that cometh to Me I will in no wise cast out' (John 6:37). Such a promise is like music to the seeking sinner's ear, but there is more to be learned when we take the verse in full: '*All that the Father giveth Me shall come to Me*; and him that cometh to Me I will in no wise cast out.' This makes the case for our reception by the Saviour stronger than ever. We are the Father's gift to the Son.

As a result of this, another thought arises in our minds, namely, that if we are gifts from the Father to the Son, then there must be more to our spiritual awakening and pilgrimage than we had imagined. It is a humbling realisation to recognise the truth that God Himself is the prime mover in all this process. It is God who visits the sanctuary of the soul and changes its entire disposition. He establishes life and holiness there in the very depth of the soul. Louis Berkhof in his *Systematic Theology* describes clearly and spiritually the gracious initial act which sets the sinner on his way to salvation and peace with God through our Lord Jesus Christ:

'Regeneration is that act of God by which the principle of the new life is implanted in man, and the governing disposition of the soul is made holy, and the first holy exercise of this new disposition is secured.'

Regeneration is an independent, sovereign act of God performed in the sanctuary of the soul, so that in a very real sense there is a change of heart. Soon, in response to the preaching of the Word, the whole soul is in motion: mind, emotions and will directed to Christ Jesus, the only hope of salvation. It is a silent, invisible work in the subconscious, but soon it will make itself known in a new appetite for the things of God. Because it is an independent, sovereign act of God, from then onwards nothing can be the same again. Once a work of grace has begun in the soul it will eventually come to its happy conclusion. We have moved from death to life. Only God can change the course of our souls away from a miserable destination and direct us to Himself and to a glorious end. The awakened soul and enlightened mind quickly make their way to the blessed Saviour to be justified in the sight of a holy God, through His costly and precious work for us. We shall never in this life fully understand the mystery of His mercy towards His people. It is sufficient that we are grateful to know that 'He doeth all things well'.

The gracious work in a sinner's soul is also called the *rebirth*, since by it we enter into the new life in Christ. Our direction in life is changed and everything is new: 'Therefore if any man be in Christ, he is a new creature: old things are passed away; behold, all things are become new' (2 Corinthians 5:17). The life of God has begun in us and great is our privilege. Heaven rejoices and we are eternally glad.

Some years ago I worked as an art master in a day

school and I found there was so much to be learned by observing the children. For example, suppose the task for a certain lesson would be to paint a scene with some figures in the foreground and hilly countryside as the background. If the children were left to work as they wanted, most of them would paint the figures first and then endeavour to fill in the background scene around them. The result was total confusion, with a clash of colours and blank spaces because the picture had not been correctly composed. The class needed to be taught to paint the background first in pale shades and then to add the foreground details in bolder colours.

There is a lesson we can learn from this illustration. Let the figures in the foreground represent ourselves, the Saviour and Satan. There is a conflict in progress. One moment we listen to the whisperings of Satan telling us that we will be joyless and miserable if we follow Jesus. The next moment we are drawn by the Saviour's love and His offer of life to the sinner who comes to Him. If this was a moving picture it would show Satan being rejected and the Saviour embraced, and at that point there would be no doubt over our own responsibility in our responding and coming to the Saviour. With Horatius Bonar we would truly say:

I came to Jesus as I was,
Weary, and worn, and sad;
I found in Him a resting-place,
And He has made me glad.

Those lines seem to express quite rightly how 'I' was totally involved; but then there is a tap on my shoulder and a voice asks me to turn around and take a closer look at those mountains in the background. I am informed that they are called the range of God's sovereign grace and each peak has its own name. There is the mountain of the great purposes of God; there is the mount of election, and of providence, and of God's holy will; another of predestination, and of love, and of mercy; and so on and on. I stand amazed at these vast and lofty mountains and I begin to realise that there was much more to my salvation than the experience of conflict and commitment. God was involved in this before the foundation of the world. The nearer I draw to those mountains of grace, the surer and firmer my assurance becomes, yet I never forget the happy day that fixed my choice on my Saviour.

But that is only a simple illustration taken from painting. The full picture of God's grace is far more wonderful and glorious, such is the assurance and reassurance that is ours in Him:

> For I am persuaded, that neither death, nor life, nor angels, nor principalities, nor powers, nor things present, nor things to come, nor height, nor depth, nor any other creature, shall be able to separate us from the love of God, which is in Christ Jesus our Lord (Romans 8:38-39).

So begins what Henry Scougal aptly called 'The Life of God in the Soul of Man'. Those who have this life can be sure that God who 'hath begun a good work in you will perform it' (Philippians 1:6). How this happens will be unfolded in subsequent chapters. This is the wonder of His work in us, His people.

2

Sanctification

*'That ye might walk worthy of the Lord unto all
pleasing, being fruitful in every good work,
and increasing in the knowledge of God'*
(Colossians 1:10).

Nothing short of heaven itself could be more wonderful than the experience of a soul finding the Saviour and receiving the sweet assurance of sins forgiven and a place reserved in glory. When that happens, then nothing can really be the same again for that person. As well as a change of destination, there is a change of direction in life.

A Christian is indeed a new creation (2 Corinthians 5:17). In a certain respect the old life is over and done with. This does not mean that we sever ourselves from our family, our friends and associates, but rather our love and concern for them take on a different dimension. It is our hope that they will begin to see a difference in us as we follow our walk with God, and as we have the joy of knowing that we belong to Him.

As we saw in the previous chapter, it is when God

sends the Holy Spirit into our hearts and quickens us
that everything changes. The principle of new life is
implanted in the very sanctuary of the soul and a new
disposition, a holy one, is established there.

Then follows an essential response as we come to
Christ and find Him to be a glorious Saviour who has
met the requirements of God's law in a two-fold way,
which has been described as His active and His
passive obedience. In His active obedience He fulfilled for us all the requirements of the law in His
perfect life. In His passive obedience He took upon
Himself our failure to comply with God's holy will
and paid the penalty of our disobedience to God's law
in full. The penalty for our sin was put to His account,
that is, imputed to Him as He took our place and was
punished in our stead. Then His excellence and His
righteousness of His perfect life are counted for us
and imputed to us. He lived a life for us that we could
never have lived, and died a death in which we would
be forever paying the penalty.

From then onwards we walk with the Lord and are
led by the Holy Spirit, that same Spirit which awakened us from the slumber of death and brought us to
Christ. Our Lord describes the new life as a narrow
way (Matthew 7:14). It is a worthwhile life consistent
with the will of God, and it is a life that is well-
pleasing in His sight.

It is important to realise that when we read that
without holiness we shall not see God (Hebrews
12:14), we are not to think that it means that our
progress depends on our adherence to a system of
rigorous rules so that by our own efforts we can find

our way to God. What it does mean is that the life of
God should be increasingly apparent in us, and this is
a two-sided process. The first side is that God perse-
veres with us and patiently shows us the way He
wants us to follow. The second side calls for our
strenuous and joyful co-operation, yet remembering
all the time that the strength we need comes from God
Himself. This is why we are encouraged to 'work out
[our] own salvation with fear and trembling. For it is
God which worketh in [us] both to will and to do of
His good pleasure' (Philippians 2:12-13). Here we
find the balance between God's sovereign will and
power and our own responsibility as Christians.

The Christian life is often described as *growing in
grace*, and it is true to say that at first we are as new-
born babes who should then become children and
eventually mature believers. Because it is a life of
fellowship with God, inevitably the influences of
God's pure and perfect character will have a significant effect.

When a happily married couple have lived together for many years, they become very similar in
their outlook and it is quite evident that they understand each other very well, so much so that they know
exactly the feelings and reactions of one another in
different situations. This is a beautiful illustration of
a harmonious unity, yet with the partners retaining a
separate identity and personality of their own.

On a higher, spiritual level, our walk with God
should increasingly manifest a sweet harmony of
fellowship and unity between the Lord and the believer. Even so the individual does not become some

kind of spiritual 'clone', but still retains his own interesting and unique identity. I am not sure that it is true, but I was told as a child that no two snowflakes are exactly identical; I suspect that it would take centuries to prove the case. But I do believe that there are no two individuals exactly the same. We are all different and we are all special. This is why we are given individual attention, since God Himself takes a personal interest in each believer.

I can illustrate this from my own experience some years ago when I needed constant medical attention over a prolonged period. Together with many others I was placed under the care and supervision of a very able and considerate doctor. In his own sphere he was world famous, yet to us, his patients, he was a most humble person and I came to regard him as a close friend because he made me feel special. The time came, however, for his retirement and his patients arranged a farewell meeting to present a gift as a mark of our appreciation. Towards the end of the meeting, when he got up to speak, a very remarkable thing happened. The whole crowd moved forward to shake his hand and embrace him. Never before or since have I seen such a touching and demonstrative show of love by a wide cross-section of people from a variety of backgrounds. Yet my first reaction was to feel a strange unwillingness in the discovery that they were all special to him. It was then that I realised what a remarkable man he was. His heart was large enough to contain us all, without depriving any of his atten-tion and care. I shall always remember him with warmth and gratitude. Yet on a far higher level, the psalmist writes that 'the Lord thinketh upon me' (Psalm 40:17).

It is a staggering fact that the God of creation, perfect in all His attributes and all His ways, is aware of me! The God who knows of the fall of a sparrow and the hairs of our heads, certainly knows of the tremors of our hearts. We are in His hands, and He gives us His undivided attention. In a society that cares little and a world that seems to grow ever harder, God's loving-kindness and tender care remain the same. He is totally interested and involved in our spiritual progress.

> God, who made the earth,
> The air, the sky, the sea,
> Who gave the light its birth,
> Careth for me.   *Sarah Betts Rhodes*

The Christian is aware that something has happened to him and that his relationship with God is a lasting one. The Holy Spirit will be our guide and teacher along this narrow way as God works out His purposes for us in His own way, forever improving and forever refining us by His grace. Although our position always remains the same, our progression continues all the days of our lives.

On a coin, one side has the head of the sovereign or head of state stamped on it and the other will have some relevant impression pertaining to the life of that nation. If this example is applied to us as Christians, on one side of the coin of our spiritual experience is the head of our Lord. This will represent our position in Christ, that is, the fact that our sin and unrighteousness have been imputed to, or put upon, Christ and the penalty has been paid by Him on our behalf. As well as this, His perfect life which satisfied God's law is counted for us, as if we had lived such a gracious life. This righteousness of Christ is put to our account. Thus our position is totally secure and as a result the impression of our Lord is firmly stamped on one side of our spiritual coin.

But if this has happened then the other side must not remain blank. There will be spiritual activity in which we are closely involved as we co-operate with God's plan for us, and are enabled and helped by the Holy Spirit. How kind God is, in that even on this side of the spiritual coin He helps us constantly. This side of our coin can be called our progression in grace.

In summary, it can be briefly described in this way. On one side is the imputed (put on us) righteousness of Christ for the believer; on the other side is the imparted (worked in us) righteousness of Christ. We must make every effort to ensure that this other side has a clear story of grace to tell.

In the sixth chapter of the Epistle to the Romans there is a vivid description of this spiritual work of sanctifying or making the believer more like the Saviour. In order to appreciate it we need to pause for a moment and consider the great change that God has wrought in us to make us Christians.

If the heart is regarded as the very spirit or sanctuary of the soul, then this will be a help in understanding the fundamentals of this teaching. The Scriptures tell us what we are like in no uncertain terms: 'And God saw that the wickedness of man was great in the earth, and that every imagination of the thoughts of his heart was *only evil continually*' (Genesis 6:5). Nothing less than a change of heart can cause such a soul to follow God.

This change of heart happens in our new birth or quickening: 'But God, who is rich in mercy, for His great love wherewith He loved us, even when we were dead in sins, hath quickened us together with Christ (by grace ye are saved)' (Ephesians 2:4-5). This change of heart influences our total direction, not only in that initial and most blessed journey to our Saviour and our salvation, but also for the remainder of our days.

God's influence will be actively felt in our faculties. In our *minds* there is a deeper understanding of spiritual things, and this enlightenment is progressive. Even our *memories* are controlled with a cleansing influence which helps us not to dwell on that which is unworthy. Our *affections* are set on those things which are above. There is most certainly a difference in our *conscience*, which now becomes alert and sensitive to God's character and ways. The *will* as a result of being in God's hands is able to make decisions in a thoughtful and spiritual manner about the great things and the little things in life. It is small wonder that this significant change occupies all our days and all our being.

We can now appreciate more fully the expressive

description in Romans 6:6: 'Knowing this, that our old man is crucified with Him, that the body of sin might be destroyed, that henceforth we should not serve sin.' This shows that the seat of authority, the very heart of the soul, has undergone a transformation so that we are able to say that our old man is crucified with Christ and we have become new. This change of heart does not mean a loss of personal identity, but a change of disposition, to one that is holy and inclined towards God.

Although no illustration can convey the full impact of the change which is the key to the on-going work of sanctification, let us imagine a school that is in a really bad condition. The Head Teacher can represent the heart or spirit of the soul and the main faculties of the soul can be represented by five classes. The children in these classes would then manifest the activities in the life of the soul.

In our example, the Head Teacher shows no interest in his duties and stays in his room behind a desk piled high with unattended letters and papers. Not surprisingly there is a state of total chaos amongst the children and pandemonium reigns in the classrooms.

Then one day the Director of Education visits the school and spends some time talking with the Head Teacher. Next morning there is a striking difference in the Head's appearance and attitude, and the children and staff hardly recognise this spruce figure, some even exclaiming that he seems like a new man.

He at once calls a staff meeting, though the five

teachers are late arriving and are very unco-operative in their manner. The Head kindly informs them of his change of heart and explains that from now on the school will be run according to the wishes and desires of the Director of Education. The staff smile, as if they know this new outlook will not last long, and prepare to express their own opinions. However, although the Head's tone suggested there was nothing to discuss, he does invite their comments.

Mr. Mind, who was in charge of the top class, says that he believes in complete liberty of thought and he should therefore have licence to think and act as he likes. In reply the Head points out that such an attitude produces chaos, and quietly recommends a new principle: 'Casting down imaginations, and every high thing that exalteth itself against the knowledge of God, and bringing into captivity every thought to the obedience of Christ' (2 Corinthians 10:5).

Next to speak is Mr. Memory, who feels highly embarrassed with his past record, but who says that he cannot see any way the present system could be changed into a clear and orderly curriculum. The Head quietly answers: 'Set your affections on things above, not on things on the earth' (Colossians 3:2).

At this Mr. Affections looks very upset and states that he does not believe it is possible to direct the affections, let alone the passions, from unworthy things to things of eternal value.

Then Mr. Conscience, who has been dreaming of retirement for some time, seems to wake up as if stirred by the first pangs of remorse, especially as the

Head says: 'Let us draw near with a true heart in full
assurance of faith, having our hearts sprinkled from
an evil conscience, and our bodies washed with pure
water' (Hebrews 10:22).

At last, Mr. Will has his say and tries to defend his
selfish decisions in the past; but when he finishes the
Head simply replies: 'Wherefore be ye not unwise,
but understanding what the will of the Lord is'
(Ephesians 5:17).

By this time the staff all accept that the new
system is right and good; but when it comes to facing
the children in their classes, what then? The school
has been in a chaotic state for so long! The Head
assures them that he will give each class his personal
attention whenever necessary and reminds them that
all the power and resources of the Director of Education are behind them in their task.

The illustration is a simple one but it displays the
areas of obedience and submission to the authority of
God and His Word. He is the great, divine Director of
Education. Yet in some ways the illustration only
touches the surface of the true position. There is so
much work to be done, so much debris to be cleared
away, so much to be unlearned and dismissed before
the constructive work can begin. Yet in the end a
good school will emerge, and likewise in the spiritual
realm once the work has begun, it will be completed:
'Being confident of this very thing, that He which
hath begun a good work in you will perform (perfect)
it until the day of Jesus Christ' (Philippians 1:6).

As this great, progressive work of sanctification

continues, the Christian will be aware of God's activity in his life, especially on those occasions when He has restrained or rescued him in some remarkable way. However there will be many times when God intervenes and the believer is totally unaware of His protecting and preserving grace at work. Even so, whether we are aware of it or not, God is there in every situation, and since the process involves us fully it calls for determination and strenuous effort on our part.

The verses quoted earlier from Philippians 2:12-13 are the key to understanding this gracious balance. We are encouraged to work out our own salvation, but at the same time to remember that it is God who works in us, both to will and to do of His good pleasure. This is a very helpful statement and it is not difficult to see how these opposites can both be true, insofar as our limited understanding goes. It makes good sense that we should pause, as it were, and think the matter through with all its implications for us as Christians. In other words, we have to learn to think spiritually and to realise that working out our salvation involves our entire behaviour as Christians, namely, our sanctification.

Clearly this does not mean doing what I think is best according to my own standards. It requires submission to the authority of Scripture as we are guided by the Holy Spirit. Furthermore it is essential that we get this right because we are responsible in that great day of Christ when we will be answerable as Christians for the application of God's grace in our lives.

At the same time, although we may have worked
out how we should react and respond as Christians in
various circumstances, the fulfilling of the task may
daunt us. It is then that we have the assurance of the
underlying promise of God that we shall be given
both the will and the ability to carry out by His
strength what is so well pleasing in His sight. Nothing
pleases Him more than to see His children walking
with Him in perfect obedience, harmony and peace.

There are many passages of Scripture which describe this spiritual progression and this growth in
grace, and which are intended to help us so that in our
daily lives we may become increasingly Christlike.

For example, Paul in his Letter to the Church at
Ephesus records two prayers (1:15-23; 3:14-21) that
he has been praying for the Christians there. Both
prayers are beautiful and helpful. As far as sanctification is concerned, the second one is particularly
helpful, and it has been described by Charles Simeon
as the 'celestial ladder'. This is an apt phrase because
it conveys the thought of the Christian life ascending
gradually like a ladder leading up to heaven itself.
The prayer takes us step by step in this spiritual
adventure of grace. Paul is careful to begin by referring to the family of believers and addressing his
prayer to our heavenly Father. So the ladder is firmly
established on redemption ground, and Paul reminds
us that to make progress in the Christian life it is vital
to draw on the limitless resources of God for every
believer. As Annie Flint, the hymnist, writes:

His love has no limit, His grace has no measure,
His power has no boundary known unto men;
For out of His infinite riches in Jesus
He giveth, and giveth, and giveth again.

The first request, or the first rung on the ladder, is
to be strengthened in the inner man: 'That He would
grant you, according to the riches of His glory, to be
strengthened with might by His Spirit in the inner
man' (verse 16). That secret place, the sanctuary of
the soul where God began a work, is to be prepared
for what God has in mind for His child, and therefore
it needs to be reinforced in order to receive so much
from God.

The second step on the ladder then makes it clear
to us what this strengthening is all about: 'That Christ
may dwell in your hearts by faith' (verse 17). But we
may ask, surely we are already in Christ because of
that great relationship that we have with our Lord and
Saviour? Yes, there is the great eternal fact of salvation
that is unalterable and that is a reality to us in our
spiritual rebirth. However, the apostle here is speaking
of Christ *in* us. He is referring to the experimental and
experiential sphere, when our true desire is for the
Lord Jesus to live, guide and rule in our hearts. This
is a desire of which we should be increasingly conscious as we go on in the things of God. Nevertheless
for this reality to be true in us, not only must we be
strengthened in the very sanctuary of the soul but
there may still be remnants of sin lurking in the recesses
which must be removed if we are to benefit from this
great privilege. All this is by faith in the Lord.

The next rung of the ladder brings us to a new
dimension of love. We have already known of the
love of Christ in our salvation but in this realm there
is always more to know: 'that ye, being rooted and
grounded in love' (verse 17). It is the prayer of Paul
that every believer should advance in this quality of
divine love which will lead them to further heights.

The natural result of this is a fellowship of the
saints or believers in a very real and definite way.
Paul prays that we should be rooted and grounded in
love in order that we 'may be able to comprehend
with all saints what is the breadth, and length, and
depth, and height; and to know the love of God which
passeth knowledge' (verse 18-19). There is no contradiction in wanting us to comprehend something
which passes knowledge, because Paul is showing
that this love to which we are being led is immeasurable. Surely the breadth of God's love reaches the
furthermost corners of the earth. It is also immeasurable in its *quality* as well as its quantity since no
matter what the depth of human sin, His love can
make the foulest clean. Further still, the height of this
love rises to reach its destination in the realms of
glory. Such love will see us safely home to God
Himself. No wonder the apostle wants us to know this
love thoroughly, and no wonder he says that it passes
knowledge.

To ascend to this level of the ladder brings us to a
sensitive and tender area which is almost like a new
discovery concerning the very heart of things. How
else can this love of God be described, for indeed it

passes all understanding and sweeps us into the heart
and the glory of God, and we are lost in wonder, love
and praise. This is the divine love which brought His
Son down to redeem sinful people and we are allowed
to touch and feel its beauty.

The next statement brings us to the top rungs of
the ladder and leaves us standing in awe, because the
apostle desires 'that ye might be filled with all the
fulness of God' (verse 19). Such a thought causes us
to tremble as we ask how can mere mortals be filled
with such a fulness. It is true that we cannot contain
God or any of those attributes and qualities that
belong to Him uniquely. But God also has qualities
that can be communicated to us, and to which we can
relate. Even though they dwell in perfection in Him,
we may touch their perimeter. This is how these
qualities are described by Charles Simeon:

'The apostle's prayer rises at every successive step.
Till he comes to a height of experience which, if it had
not been dictated by inspiration, we should have been
ready to condemn as blasphemy. There is indeed in the
Deity an essential fulness which is incommunicable to
His creatures. But there is also a fulness which He does
and will communicate. In Him are all the perfections of
wisdom and goodness and justice and mercy, of patience, of love, of truth and fruitfulness, and with these
He will fill His people according to the measure of his
capacity, so that they shall be holy as He is holy, and
perfect as their Father which is in heaven is perfect. But
how is this to be attained? Will repentance effect it?
No. Will mortification procure it? No. That which
alone will avail for this is an enlarged discovery of the

love of Christ. Therefore the apostle prays for one in
order to have the other. How much do the saints in
general live below their privileges?'

Paul draws his prayer to a conclusion with comforting words. If his prayer had ended with the phrase
considered previously we would look on almost with
despair. How could I climb such a ladder, or reach
such dizzy heights? Our hearts would fail within us,
were we not led to the next verse: 'Now unto Him that
is able to do exceeding abundantly above all that we
ask or think, according to the power that worketh in
us' (verse 20).

Paul reminds us that there is a divine power at
work in us. It is this power of God that inspires and
enables us to perform His will in a way above our
asking. Think of it! The abundant grace of God upon
us and within us, persevering with us, and refining
our hearts and our lives. He has in view that we should
be men and women of grace. Yet all the way it is a stiff
climb and it calls for our generous co-operation in the
glorious work of grace.

Sometimes we have to stand back and take a long
look at life as we seriously consider what we desire
most. Above all the little wants and desires in our
lives there is a greater hunger, a hunger and thirst
after righteousness, a longing for God Himself.

> Enthrone thy God within thy heart,
> Thy being's inmost shrine;
> He doth to thee the power impart
> To live the life divine.

Seek truth in Him with Christlike mind;
With faith His will discern;
Walk on life's way with Him, and find
Thy heart within thee burn.

With love that overflows thy soul
Love Him who first loved thee;
Is not His love thy life, thy goal,
Thy soul's eternity?

Serve Him in His sufficing strength:
Heart, mind and soul employ;
And He shall crown thy days at length
With everlasting joy.   *William Joseph Penn*

3

Providence

'Yet the Lord thinketh upon me'
(Psalm 40:17).

One very beautiful facet of the Christian faith is the teaching regarding the providence of God. This means that God is not only the great architect of our salvation but that He cares for His people as they live their Christian lives through all the mass of circumstances which await them on their earthly pilgrimage. The Scriptures are full of references that assure us of God's loving kindness and His tender mercy, and that underneath us are the everlasting arms. We are encouraged to cast all our cares upon the Lord for He cares for us (1 Peter 5:7). This is because we have entered into a relationship in which the Lord is deeply involved. If He is aware of the fall of a sparrow or the number of hairs on our head, it is not difficult to conclude that He knows of, and is concerned for, every flutter of anxiety that we feel, and that He would have us not be anxious over anything. It is a profound comfort to know that our lives are not a haphazard jumble of events, but that God is in all and is working out His purposes and plans. We are in His care. One of the old divines, commenting on the verse in the first epistle of Peter which says that we have 'an inheritance incorruptible, and undefiled, and that fadeth not away, reserved in heaven for us', added that the saints are preserved for a place reserved for them.

A more formal description of providence is well worth examining. For example, it is described in the works of the theologian Louis Berkhof in this way:

> 'Providence may be defined as that continued exercise of the divine energy whereby the Creator preserves all His creatures, is operative in all that comes to pass in the world and directs all things to their appointed end.'

This statement distinguishes three elements in providence: preservation, co-operation and government. The statement may sound a little remote, yet when we consider that it describes the energetic activity of God that is constantly involved with His people, this should encourage us at all times, even when it seems that everything has gone wrong and that nobody cares. It is then that we must remember God, and think of His chosen interest in every one of His children. However difficult the way may be, God is there.

> I know not what may soon betide,
> Or how my wants shall be supplied;
> But Jesus knows, and will provide.   *John Newton*

God is sovereign, and it therefore follows that nothing can be outside His jurisdiction and His providential care, particularly for those who have believed in His Son, Jesus Christ. The power behind this preserving and sustaining care shown by God has no limit and cannot be frustrated. This is God's right.

Our response to the will of God must be real. He calls for our generous co-operation in all spiritual matters and for a consistent Christian life. Yet behind this lifestyle is the supporting hand of God and we need to be mindful that He governs – for we live, move and have our being in total dependence upon God. The Christian life is one where God is totally involved with us and we are totally involved with Him. We belong to Him, for in a very special way we are His property.

God's providence in truth and experience

Paul, in writing his epistles, would sometimes emphasise a particular point by saying that he 'knew' it; in other words, there was no argument or doubt that the statement was spiritually reliable. For example, the eighth chapter of Romans contains truths that are profoundly moving, and from the very beginning it leaves the reader in no doubt as to who is being addressed: 'There is therefore now no condemnation to them which are in Christ Jesus' (8:1). Then follows a succession of magnificent truths until the chapter reaches the great climax which describes the believer as a person who is inseparable from the love of God in Christ Jesus. As part of that climax there is this crucial statement: 'And we know that all things work

together for good to them that love God, to them who
are the called according to His purpose' (Romans
8:28).

When we look back over our lives there are so
many memories that we can recall. We each have our
share of sad memories, of hard times which may
include the loss of a loved one, disappointment in
friends, or being passed over when possibly we were
the better person for a post or even for office in the
church itself. We also have our share of joys in our
families and loved ones, and in the many examples of
thoughtfulness and kindness that gladden our memories.

Also, no doubt, we all have our share of failures
when we have let the Lord down, or have become
weary and despaired of ourselves. At such times
Satan does not lose his opportunities to rub salt into
the wounds. Yet, nevertheless, our position in Christ
remains the same through it all:

> When Satan tempts me to despair,
> And tells me of the guilt within,
> Upward I look, and see Him there
> Who made an end of all my sin.
>
> *Charitie Lees De Chenez*

We should not forget those times when we have been
severely tempted, when we have drawn our strength
from God and have been enabled to overcome a
wrong attitude or a sin. At such moments our joy has
been full and the memory should cherish these occasions of spiritual victory.

In addition, our memories of past experiences are often bound up with the various circumstances in which we have found ourselves. To some there may have been the constant problem of limited resources or even poverty, while others face the problem of how to handle riches, keenly aware of their answerability to God. There are those who have the care of a sick child or an ageing relative, where they have to lay aside their own lives to a great extent. Some people seem always to have enjoyed health and strength – how vital then to be daily grateful for such kindnesses from the Lord our God. Conversely, others have been physically limited or seem never to be out of the clutches of ill-health. How essential it is then to have that most excellent spirit which was attributed to Daniel by a pagan queen (Daniel 5:12). And so we could go on, each of us filling in our own story with its ups and downs, its moments of joy and sorrow, its times of happiness and even despair. In such a world as this where nations collapse and people fear and tremble, we cannot take anything for granted. Oh yes we can! God is always there, 'for He hath said, I will never leave thee, nor forsake thee' (Hebrews 13:5).

In our key verse (Romans 8:28) we are told that 'all things' are being taken into consideration. Now we could the more easily accept that some things in life appear beneficial, and out of a selected few items we could find some that were for our good. However, this amazing God insists that He means 'all things' and Paul, led by the Holy Spirit, tells us that he *knows* this.

An illustration by an old Welsh preacher makes the point clear. He described the eastern and western coastlines of South America and noted that on the west side was the Pacific Ocean, which by reputation and name is generally peaceful, yet on whose shore the rocks are sharp and jagged so that it is impossible to walk on them. On the eastern side the rocks are smooth and kind to the feet because their rough edges have been eroded by the storms of the Atlantic.

I am not sure how true that illustration is, but God does have His own ways of taking our critical spirit, our sharp tongue or our bitterness over something or other, and causing us to be well-refined by His grace. The Lord is always working on His people and never allows anything to go to waste, even if it is a bitter lesson. Peter, when writing to the scattered Christians suffering for their faith under the rule of the cruel Roman emperor Nero, stated that they were

'kept by the power of God through faith unto salvation ready to be revealed in the last time. Wherein ye greatly rejoice, though now for a season, if need be, ye are in heaviness through manifold temptations (afflictions): that the trial of your faith, being much more precious than of gold that perisheth, though it be tried with fire, might be found unto praise and honour and glory at the appearing of Jesus Christ' (1 Peter 1:5-7).

No matter what situation a Christian may be in, Paul states that 'all things work together for good'. This is astounding news! Let us imagine that we are sitting in the depths of despondency and disillusionment, and then we become aware of the presence of God. His gracious promises flood into our mind, and we know that He cares and that we are not on our own. He is sitting there with me and kindly and gently, yet firmly, He takes my hand and helps me to stand and to realise that in some mysterious way my situation will work out for good. He may let me know a little now, but one day He will show me the whole pattern as I look back –from the hills of the heavenly Zion – over the sharp bends and twists of my pilgrimage through life. But for the present He encourages me to trust Him.

> Who trusts in God, a strong abode
> In heaven and earth possesses;
> Who looks in love to Christ above,
> No fear his heart oppresses.
> In Thee alone, dear Lord, we own
> Sweet hope and consolation,
> Our shield from foes, our balm from woes,
> Our great and sure salvation.
>
> Though Satan's wrath beset our path,
> And worldly scorn assail us,
> While Thou art near we will not fear,
> Thy strength shall never fail us.
> Thy rod and staff shall keep us safe,
> And guide our steps for ever;
> Nor shades of death, nor hell beneath,
> Our souls from Thee shall sever.
>
> In all the strife of mortal life
> Our feet shall stand securely;

Temptation's hour shall lose its power,
For Thou shall guard us surely.
O God, renew, with heavenly dew,
Our body, soul and spirit,
Until we stand at Thy right hand,
Through Jesus' saving merit.

(verse 1 Joachim Magdeburg; verses 2-3
Anonymous, tr. by Benjamin Hall Kennedy)

The goodness of God's providence takes all things in His hands and works them for our eternal good. He is always preparing us for that time when we shall walk with Him in unbroken fellowship of holiness and love. We must always remember that we are His workmanship and this should call for our glad response. God is good and His purposes for His people are good. Moreover, it is God alone who can perform and perfect such work: 'Being confident of this very thing, that He which hath begun a good work in you will perform it until the day of Jesus Christ' (Philippians 1:6). We can be assured that our Lord will not give us up or grow weary of His task in us. He will complete it.

Who are these fortunate people in whom the Lord will carry out such a gracious work? In the same verse in Romans we are given a beautiful balance of spiritual reality: 'to them who are the called according to His purpose'. A Christian is able to say that he loves God, especially when he recognises the initial love that brought the Lord Jesus Christ into this world to die for our sins and also to fulfil God's law in our place. We have every reason to love God with a true

and spontaneous love for He is everything to us. This
appreciation of our Lord has been expressed in so
many ways, such as *Jesus, Thou joy of loving hearts*
or

> How sweet the Name of Jesus sounds
> In a believer's ear!
> It soothes his sorrows, heals his wounds,
> And drives away his fear.   *John Newton*

We realise that our love is a response to His love
to us, yet it is *our* love. This love for God in our hearts
produces a radiant and a joyous life. When we love
God, we trust and we know, like Paul, that the Lord
has only our eternal good in mind.

The verse also explains the *nature* of such love
and its source. On our side, in our love towards Him
there is the genuine effort of our heart, but on the
other side of the coin is the fact that we are the result
of God's call to our souls. The recipients of such care
are described as those who not only love God but also
have been called by Him. Here is a reference to that
call to the awakened soul which is a call to faith in our
Lord and Saviour Jesus Christ. This direct and special call invites the soul residing in the midst of the
worst unbelief to respond. It is able to do so because
the secret work of the Holy Spirit in awakening that
soul has taken place.

The last phrase in this verse – 'who are the called
according to His purpose' – is very significant. All
this activity has happened because it is part of the
plan and purpose of God. Behind it all, there is the

hand of God. This is no patched up job but a thorough and permanent work of God in our souls. Surely our hearts are thrilled to realise that it is the determined will of God to perform such a work in us that will manifest His goodness and be for our eternal benefit.

Even so, we cannot overlook the fact that in life we will often be surrounded by many discouragements. The wiles of Satan will ensure that he is forever devising means to cause us to stumble, whether it is by deception as an angel of light or a minister of righteousness, or by fear as a roaring lion seeking whom he may devour. But as well as that, there is the lust within us for old ways which die hard, and oftentimes this can cause us to revert to former habits and attitudes. A powerful force in life is wielded by our peers, who have little interest in godliness and lay all their store upon material possessions and self-importance. The magnetic influence of these acquaintances can so easily draw us aside and we slip under the tyranny of things and the ambitions of the flesh. How can we be kept, and what promises has God for us in such a world as this?

The answer is, and must always be, that we must not cease to be aware of the greatness of God's sovereignty, and that His greatness not only encompasses and controls the universe and the endless beyond, but it is also concerned with every one of His people. There is a personal relationship with Him that reaches the frailest of His children. We must never forget our position for, as new creations in Christ, we are His ongoing workmanship and each soul is as

precious as another to Him. We matter to Him for He
cares.

Be careful for nothing

There will still be times, even knowing and appreci-
ating these great truths of God's providential care,
when life threatens to overwhelm us. There may be
adverse circumstances and events, or difficulties that
never seem to go away and that wear us into the
ground. Sometimes we hardly know what they are
but we feel like weary little pilgrims who have taken
a great battering on the way. Even the experience of
loneliness by itself, without any particular problem,
can weigh us down, while others we know are surrounded with family and friends and seem so happy.
Whatever its cause, there is such a thing as being full
of care and feeling badly about it because we say to
ourselves that we should not be like this.

It is possible to know the answer for our difficulties, and yet not be able or not even to think of
applying the grace and the help that the Lord is so
ready to give. At such times it is good to take one
relevant portion of Scripture which includes a promise from God and to lay hold upon it. We are instructed by God to ask and seek, but it is always the
Lord that grants that enabling grace. When Paul
wrote to that gracious and generous church at Philippi
he said:

> 'Be careful for nothing; but in every thing by prayer
> and supplication with thanksgiving let your requests

be made known unto God. And the peace of God which passeth all understanding, shall keep your hearts and minds through Christ Jesus' (Philippians 4:6-7).

The instructions are quite clear. We are told not to be anxious or full of care about anything. How easy it is to make an exception and put some worry in brackets, immediately nullifying any comfort we could have received. 'Nothing' means nothing. It may well be the beginning of understanding to recognise that we have nothing when we come to Him. Let me use a simple illustration.

When I was a child it took me a long time to understand the mysteries of mathematics. On a particular day my class was having a test. We were given four problems to solve and then told to exchange papers with the person sitting next to us. Then we had to put a tick or a cross as the answers were given by the teacher. I duly exchanged my paper with a little boy whom I had hitherto regarded as my friend! He had one correct answer out of four, for which he was awarded four marks, so that his result was four out of sixteen. However I had none right, which made a total of nought out of sixteen. I meekly accepted this as reality.

We were then shown how to work out our results in percentages and that was when the confusion started. My friend's four marks leapt to an incredible twenty-five percent! Twenty-one points had appeared as a free gift! Then to my utter consternation my nought remained nought! I felt it was grossly unfair. I protested to the teacher and stated my case, but she simply said that she could understand from my arguments why I had scored nought.

I then asked permission to appeal to the headmaster, which she patiently allowed. He in turn asked me what I had in my hand, to which I promptly answered 'one nothing'. He repeated this four times and then asked what was the total in my hand. He expected me to say 'nothing' but I insisted that I had 'four nothings'. It was much later that I learned that nothing means nothing and it never changes. You cannot alter it by any mathematical means.

As Christians, we are told not to be anxious, but somehow or another we make exceptions and continue on our harassed little way.

The peace of God

The next phrase in this verse of Paul's Letter to the Philippians seems to repeat this guidance but it does take us on: 'but in every thing by prayer and supplication with thanksgiving let your requests be made known unto God'. We are encouraged to come to the Lord in prayer and bring everything to Him without exception, large worries and small worries.

> O what peace we often forfeit,
> O what needless pain we bear,
> All because we do not carry
> Everything to God in prayer.
>
> *Joseph Medlicott Scriven*

We are to come with a thankful heart, mindful of

many past mercies, and make our requests known. We know them and God knows them, yet we are told to make them known to God. What does He do?

In His wisdom, our first requirement may not spring to our minds, but it is *the peace of God*. As the Lord stilled the raging wind and calmed the tempestuous sea, so He brings peace to the anxious mind and the troubled heart. All this is provided through the Lord Jesus Christ. Peace of heart and peace of mind are very rare and precious gifts. The circumstances may or may not have changed, but we have. Later, in the eleventh verse of the same chapter, Paul tells us that he had learned that Christian contentment was available whatever his situation was at the time. We must learn to avail ourselves of the generous providence of God.

This is what our God is like. He works His purposes out in storms and trials but always cares tenderly for His own. He knows exactly how much we are able to bear. The preservation of His people is taken seriously because it is His intention that they should arrive safely home at their final destination.

Great providence of heaven –
What wonders shine
In its profound display
Of God's design:
It guards the dust of earth,
Commands the hosts above,
Fulfils the mighty plan
Of His great love.
                    David Charles, tr. by Edmund Tudor Owen

4

Fellowship

'Can two walk together, except they be agreed?'
(Amos 3:3)

In the first Epistle of John, the spiritual relationship between Christians and God is described in a very special way. God is portrayed as light in order to convey the perfection of His holiness, His magnificent purity and His total integrity to His own being and His character. Anyone who claims fellowship with God and continues to live and abide in sin without any conscience or shame is surely deceiving himself. The apostle writes: 'If we say that we have fellowship with Him, and walk in darkness, we lie, and do not the truth' (1 John 1:6). Such a life would be a contradiction of the truth of the gospel and the entire concept of God's salvation.

However, those who walk by faith and in honesty of spirit with the Lord have entered into a fellowship, not only with other Christian pilgrims, but most especially with their Lord. They need not be gripped with doubts and endless self-examination, but may live simply and openly with God. A Christian can still sin, but that is a vastly different matter from walking in darkness.

When we have an assurance in our hearts that we are the children of God, we discover that there is so much more to be known and experienced in our relationship with God. It is essential that we have a sound knowledge of the fundamental truths of the gospel concerning our Lord and Saviour Jesus Christ. Coupled with this is that inner work of God the Holy Spirit imparting the knowledge within us that we are truly born of God. Yet it is necessary to point out that in order to get the best from this glorious relationship we need to have the living reality of His presence, and maintain our daily walk with Him. This has been called 'practising the presence of God', and by its very title it suggests an active participation on our part.

We have probably known godly men and women who so obviously impressed us with something of the radiance of God in their lives. By this it is not meant that they have a perpetual smile and an almost celestial shine in their eyes, which I have often found to cause me concern or even embarrassment. Rather there is a distinct impression made of the spiritual honesty of that person which convinces us that there is such a thing as spiritual reality in the daily life of a Christian – a reality that we all long for.

The questions arise: How do we go about attaining this? Is there a secret? Must we be naturally spiritual? Of course not, because by nature we are not spiritual and no-one has a running start over the other. If that were so it would depend upon our individual personality, and that would be most daunting for those who honestly desire with all their hearts to live by the grace of God a life that is well pleasing to Him, to glorify Him and to enjoy Him. We begin from where we are; we begin with God.

There are some very straightforward guidelines in this area of our spiritual life. For a start there is the important matter of *communication with God*.

Recently a telephone company used an excellent advertisement in which it persuaded people to 'keep talking'. This was of course to the company's advantage, but there is a valid point here for Christians too. In times of war if a message from the front-line was intercepted by the enemy it would often spell disaster for soldiers endeavouring to hold a lonely outpost. When the lifeline of communication with God is silent and He hardly ever hears from His children, then there is no surer sign that their hearts are cold, their lives are careless and their love for the cause of Christ has become indifferent.

Therefore, we must feed on daily spiritual bread, supplied in those times that we set aside to read our Bibles and to pray to God. The time spent with God is precious to the believer because he knows that there is always a Father's welcome waiting for him. We come with our thanksgiving and our petitions to the throne of grace, where we are told that we 'obtain mercy, and find grace to help in time of need' (Hebrews 4:16). This is our private line of communication with the Lord. We may or may not be able to stand and pray in the church prayer meeting, but we can come to Him daily and enjoy sweet fellowship with God.

There is a sense in which our reading of the Bible is informative, where for example we learn the story of the Children of Israel or follow the Gospel accounts of the life of our Saviour. But there is also a devotional aspect to our reading where God's Word speaks clearly to us. Sometimes it may be in rebuke and at other times in encouragement, but always for our good.

We must guard these times because the rush of activities can push our devotional life into a corner, and perhaps even force it out completely. We can so easily convince ourselves that we are busy doing good, but at the end of the day we have to admit we have had very little to do with God.

I remember a story I heard concerning a small family of a father and mother and their little daughter. It always delighted the father to receive an energetic and loving welcome from his daughter as she leapt into his arms and expressed her love when he returned home each day. One evening, however, the welcome was missing, but although the father was very disappointed he said nothing. As the weeks went on he was greatly saddened as he missed the affection of his daughter – until his birthday arrived.

As they sat at the tea-table the little girl produced a pair of cloth slippers she had been laboriously making for him over many weeks. She asked him excitedly, 'Do you like them, Daddy?' He answered that he liked them very much, but realising at last the reason for the missing daily welcome, he picked her up in his arms and said, 'But I'd rather have you!'

Precisely so! Our Lord delights in the adoration and fellowship of us His children more than all our gifts and offerings, lovely as they may be. God desires our fellowship and we should desire His.

It would be easy to conclude that we should keep in touch with God in prayer at regular intervals as a matter of duty, and of course such regular contact is necessary, but there is far more to it than that. We take our Lord into every part of our lives; we hide no area from Him. He is our Lord and constant companion, and in this we are never alone. In doing this we learn to cultivate a constant awareness of the Saviour. That does not mean that we are neglectful in our professional duties, since we are expected to be diligent in our daily tasks and to serve our masters well.

It means that we are always within calling distance of God, like a parent and a child. Both are aware that the parent is concerned for the well-being of the child, and so the child has a quiet sense of security in the nearness of the parent. Similarly, God has our eternal good in view and we should be consciously aware that we are in His hands. When we look at the sky at night we marvel at the vastness of His creative power, or in the light of day we wonder at the beauty of nature and of the earth around us. Behind all this we see God, but He is nearer to us than that – much, much nearer. He knows of every anxious thought and any tremor of fear that we feel, for He is in our situations in a way that no one else is able to be.

Thus far, we have considered the lines of communication and hopefully established their importance

in our lives. From this there develops what can be
described as *communion with God*. It is a consciousness of the reality of that spiritual position described
in Scripture as being 'in Christ'. As those who have
come from the darkness of unbelief into the light of
faith, we are in a secure spiritual position. All the
benefits our Lord has procured for us are ours. We
have peace with God; we are in Christ. There is also
a deeply personal consciousness that we are in fellowship with a person, with all the glory of His purity
and His beauty. It is a heart relationship which can
never be broken in any way or destroyed. We are
entering that realm where we both know and feel
what it means to be in Christ. With the hymnist
Charles Edward Mudie we can say:

> I lift my heart to Thee,
> Saviour divine;
> For Thou art all to me,
> And I am Thine.
> Is there on earth a closer bond than this,
> That my Beloved's mine and I am His?

To enjoy communion with God is the unique privilege of the Christian.

Now sadly, in the same way that we can be a
member of a family and know that it is a permanent
relationship, yet still take their love for granted and
wander off in some selfish way, so too can we neglect
our fellowship with God. Perhaps we do not always
realise the hurt we cause, but also we fail to appreciate the joys of family life we are missing. Likewise,

Christians can pursue harmless little interests which cause them to neglect God, and in that way they grieve Him. What is more, we deprive ourselves of so many beautiful things we could learn and enjoy in our fellowship with Him. The Welsh hymnist, William Williams, expresses strongly his desire to remain well established in Christ by describing the Christian groaning in his soul for more of Christ, willing to part with all he has and to undergo every hardship for this sheer joy. His hymn ends with this request:

> Give me that knowledge pure, divine,
> To know and feel that Thou art mine,
> And Thee my portion call;
> That doubts and fears may flee away,
> And faith unfeigned win the day,
> And triumph over all.

There are steps in our thinking which can help us in this practising of the presence of God. The prophet Amos states a useful principle when he writes: 'Can two walk together, except they be agreed?' (Amos 3:3). Obviously they cannot if we are talking about fellowship and communion. David in Psalm 133:1 writes about this unity and praises its great value: 'Behold, how good and how pleasant it is for brethren to dwell together in unity!' In his comparison David thinks of the sweetness of precious ointment and the freshness of dew.

We have all probably had the experience of entering a room when you could cut the atmosphere with a knife and you know that there is a storm impending.

However, think of the opposite, when there is the aroma of unity and love! Agreement inevitably means that we are at one in the great truths of the gospel, but also that we are one in purpose and in spirit. That means that it is our greatest joy and pleasure to bask in total harmony and unity with God, and to safeguard this at all costs.

Yes, it must be safeguarded since Satan is ever ready to spoil this fellowship. He is happy to bring a seed of disagreement or of anxiety when we have not always fully understood the ways of God, and that simple trust is dimmed. How easy it is to forget that all things work together for good for believers. This unity has to be actively maintained and safeguarded in order to lose nothing of its sweetness and freshness.

There is another lovely aspect to be considered and that is *the happiness and delight of this life in Christ*. Whether we look at a newly married couple or a happily married couple who have spent a lifetime together, it is always a wonderful sight to observe their delight in each other. Even greater and better is our delight in our Saviour. Without Him there would be no gospel and no hope for our immortal souls, so naturally we delight in the incarnation when He came and dwelt among us. In the mystery of His person there are two natures: His perfect humanity and His absolute deity. It is He who fulfilled God's law in our place and met the penalty of that law in our place for our failure. In His redemptive work there is both gratitude and delight of soul. Augustus Toplady expressed this so well when he wrote:

Object of my first desire,
Jesus crucified for me;
All to happiness aspire,
Only to be found in Thee:
Thee to praise, and Thee to know,
Constitute my bliss below;
Thee to see, and Thee to love,
Constitute my bliss above.

Although we have not seen the Lord whilst here
on earth, yet in some strange way our hearts are
ravished with His beauty, His purity and His whole
being. It is small wonder that believers down through
the ages have used phrases from the Song of Solomon
which refer to our Lord as the Rose of Sharon, the
Lily of the Valley and the Altogether Lovely One. It
is often good in our reading of the Gospels to medi-
tate upon the words of the Saviour, and with our
mind's eye to spiritually gaze upon the One whom we
love. When we love a person, we also have great joy
in pleasing that person, and so too our chief delight is
in doing the will of our Lord. Oftentimes we need to
check on ourselves and ask what is our chief delight,
lest some less worthy thing is encroaching on His
territory. Let us always remember: 'For ye are bought
with a price: therefore glorify God in your body, and
in your spirit, which are God's' (1 Corinthians 6:20).

In this walk with the Lord there must be *an
honesty and a transparency about us* so that we hide
nothing from Him. Imagine a stained-glass window
illuminated by the bright rays of the sun. If windows
are never cleaned and dust and grime are allowed to

gather, then the light of the sun is hindered and only dimly seen. Yet when windows are kept clean, there is nothing to dim the loveliness of the colours which shine with the radiance of the sun's rays. They are in complete harmony. Transparency indicates no deception, no hidden parts, but rather an open, honest walk with the Lord.

As mentioned at the outset of this chapter, we should always bear in mind the apostle John's description of God in all His holiness and purity as light: 'This then is the message that we have heard of Him, and declare unto you, that God is light, and in Him is no darkness at all' (1 John 1:5). This makes it quite clear that all that pertains to darkness, all that is evil, all sin and lies or deception, can have no part in God at all. In Scripture we are told that such is His purity that He cannot even look upon sin: 'Thou art of purer eyes than to behold evil, and canst not look on iniquity' (Habakkuk 1:13).

Since He is a God who is true, then *lies can have no part in Him*, nor any kind of deception. Can you imagine the gaze of God? How Peter must have felt when the Lord looked upon Him. No wonder that he wept bitterly at such a pure and penetrating gaze. The integrity of God is continually underlined in Scripture: 'In hope of eternal life, which God, that cannot lie, promised before the world began' (Titus 1:2).

Not only does God not lie, but *the reliability of His promise is absolute*, and in this case it concerns our life in glory. Our Lord Jesus Christ, in discussing His departure from this earth with His disciples, described heaven in this way: 'In my Father's house are many mansions: if it were not so, I would have told you' (John 14:2). Our Saviour would never deceive us or go back on His word.

We live in a world of double-talk and falsehood or, at best, forgotten promises, and a trail of wreckage is often left by our devious words. But with God there is none of this in any of His ways; His divine purposes never waver, neither does His will change course: 'Every good gift and every perfect gift is from above, and cometh down from the Father of lights, with whom is no variableness, neither shadow of turning' (James 1:17). That means that the Lord would never lead us on and then turn away or change His plans. Our great God, when He begins a work, will always bring it to its desired end.

There is yet another negative to consider since the Bible states, 'He cannot deny Himself' (2 Timothy 2:13). God is *faithful to His own character*. Because He is perfect, there is no need for Him to change since His perfection is total in all His abilities and His attributes. In the Scriptural details of the God of light we see described a glorious person worthy to be praised – our great eternal God.

> O enter then His gates with praise,
> Approach with joy His courts unto;
> Praise, laud, and bless His Name always,
> For it is seemly so to do.
>
> For why? the Lord our God is good;
> His mercy is for ever sure;

His truth at all times firmly stood,
And shall from age to age endure.   *William Kethe*

Thus our life in Christ is our hope, and to be with Him our ultimate joy. This desire for Him and fellowship with Him, and a determination to co-operate with the Holy Spirit in our daily lives, surely are marks and evidences of grace in our lives. We may think, 'But what do I do when I fail the Lord?' Go quickly to Him and tell Him all about it, for 'If we confess our sins, He is faithful and just to forgive us our sins, and to cleanse us from all unrighteousness' (1 John 1:9).

What an amazing gospel this is, when we consider that relationship with Christ which secures our eternal position, and that our forgiveness is total. There may still be daily failure when we seem to grow in grace so slowly or we fall into an old sin that we thought we had bidden farewell to, yet there is cleansing when we confess it before God. Our fellowship is safe but its happy intimacy has to be restored. When David failed the Lord as a believer, he cried out with a repentant heart, 'Restore unto me the joy of Thy salvation' (Psalm 51:12). Gladly and mercifully, God does!

Lord, it is not life to live
If Thy presence Thou deny;
Lord, if Thou Thy presence give,
'Tis no longer death to die:
Source and giver of repose,
Singly from Thy smile it flows;

Peace and happiness are Thine;
Mine they are, if Thou art mine.

Whilst I feel Thy love to me,
Every object teems with joy;
May I ever walk with Thee,
For 'tis bliss without alloy:
Let me but Thyself possess,
Total sum of happiness:
Perfect peace I then shall prove,
Heaven below and heaven above.   *Augustus Toplady*

5

Repentance

'The sacrifices of God are a broken spirit:
a broken and a contrite heart, O God,
Thou wilt not despise' (Psalm 51:17).

In considering the initial experience in our relationship with God – the radical change from darkness to
light, from being a child of disobedience and of wrath
to being an heir of God – it is impossible to exclude
repentance. There is no way that this can be passed by
since our dealings are with a holy God who is un-
changing in all His qualities or attributes. Sin is the
very opposite of that which God is, and sorrow for sin
and turning away from sin is an essential part of this
process of the work of grace in the soul of man in
order that there might be that sublime fellowship
which we look forward to in perfection in glory.
Without repentance for our sin, and a desire to
change, there can be no genuine relationship with
God, especially if our wish and desire is to enjoy the
presence of God in this life.

We have already considered that glorious experience when the righteousness of Christ is counted for
or imputed to us, and our sin is dealt with on the

Cross. Our standing in grace is unalterable as we are
safely placed in the finished work of Christ both in
His active obedience to the law of God in our place
and His passive obedience in paying the penalty for
our sin and failure. We are complete in Him, and this
remains unchangeably the same.

Nevertheless, in the progression of sanctification
in our lives as children of God, repentance is still an
essential ingredient. This process involves the Holy
Spirit bringing the reality of the Saviour more and
more into our experience, and encouraging our submission to the Word of God in our daily walk with
Him. Repentance is an essential part of this work.

Let me explain more fully. Early in my ministry
while I was a pastor of a country church in the heart
of the mountains of West Wales, I had many in the
congregation who were converted during the Welsh
Revival of 1904. These people were effectively known
as *Plant y Diwygiad* (the Children of the Revival). It
meant that they were the spiritual product of God's
grace in that time of sweet awakening in Wales. I had
of course met such dear saints all over Wales, but in
this case I was their minister and this gave me the
opportunity to enjoy fellowship with them and literally to learn so much from them. They still remain
precious in my heart and are an important part of my
spiritual understanding.

The point, however, is this: in our church prayer
meetings they baffled me! On the one hand they
prayed with such assurance and confidence in God as
if He were present in the room and a living reality to

them. God was the very joy of their lives. Then in the same prayers there would be such a brokenness for sin and a sense of deep unworthiness that, in my ignorance, I wondered if they had fully understood the wonderful doctrine of justification by faith in all its certainty and glory. At the same time I realised that they had such a quality of reality in all the circumstances of their lives that I longed to be like them.

As time went on I came to realise that they possessed a gentle and delicate balance between that confidence of the full assurance of faith and a profound reverence towards God which produced a sensitivity to sin that was remarkable.

Slowly I have learned that the closer we are to God, the greater is our confidence, and yet the greater is our sense of shame for the sin that lingers in our lives. Contrition of this kind is a mark of godliness.

An analogy that could be drawn is that of a child learning to play the piano. Let us spiritualise the example by imagining the child starting safely in the hands of the teacher and let that stand for the basic Christian experience with God through our Lord Jesus Christ. As the Christian begins his walk with God somewhat tentatively, so too the child in the first lessons is given simple scales to learn and similar exercises to practise. Eventually the pupil plays his first melody. To the parents of the child it seems they are listening to a maestro! Mistakes and blunders are generously overlooked until they can be patiently corrected in time. Is not our gracious Lord infinitely patient with us in the refining process of our souls?

Let us extend the illustration by imagining that the pupil becomes a famous concert pianist in adult life. By now, one false move or one note out of place ruins the performance and he is deeply conscious of any error. As we grow in grace, are we not also mortified when shades of our past behaviour creep back into our lives and we feel that we have grieved the Lord? There is always room for repentance because we are forever learners in this life of grace.

Then what is repentance and why is it so vital in our Christian life? Obviously it must be present in our first approach to God, and when coupled with faith it culminates in conversion as we avail ourselves of the immeasurable spiritual benefits in Christ that bring us into a right relationship with God. Yet the activity of repentance does not stop there since our dealings are always with a holy God. One of F. W. Faber's hymns expresses this so well as he portrays the life of the Christian endeavouring to follow the Saviour:

O how I fear Thee, living God,
With deepest, tenderest fears,
And worship Thee with trembling hope
And penitential tears.

Repentance is linked with the whole process of change. For example, it states in Acts 11:18 that God has granted the Gentiles 'repentance unto life'. There is a similar reference to repentance in the Christian's life in 2 Corinthians 7:10: 'For godly sorrow worketh repentance to salvation not to be repented of: but the sorrow of the world worketh death.'

The awakened soul in the first initial experience of God becomes aware of the fear of God, and finds repentance playing an active part. There is an inward change where the soul turns from sin to God. Repentance finds its beginnings in *a serious fear of God*. Even when the sinner is safe in the arms of justifying grace and has the forgiveness of sins and assured acceptance by God, a deep, healthy and even robust fear of God must remain. After all, He is God and dwells in depths of burning light. It is a balance of confidence and sensitivity to the awesomeness of God. Repentance and contrition of heart maintain this balance. Faber's hymn again:

> My God, how wonderful Thou art,
> Thy majesty how bright!
> How beautiful Thy mercy seat,
> In depths of burning light!
>
> How dread are Thine eternal years,
> O everlasting Lord,
> By prostrate spirits day and night
> Incessantly adored!
>
> How wonderful, how beautiful,
> The sight of Thee must be,
> Thine endless wisdom, boundless power,
> And aweful purity!

In this intimate relationship with God as He steadfastly continues His refining work in our hearts, we are aware of the privilege of being allowed fellowship with such a God. And when we do sadly fail our Lord in word or deed, it is true repentance that *restores our sweet fellowship with Him*.

Without a spirit of repentance and contrition of heart we very soon become careless in our attitude. So very quickly a familiarity creeps into our relationship with God which is far removed from the true fellowship that should be present. Furthermore, it is often followed by a carelessness in our lives that brings grief to the Holy Spirit when we so easily condone in our own behaviour what we would condemn in the lives of others. Our fellowship becomes strained and we are embarrassed in the company of the godly.

Repentance is *the key to maintaining a sweet spirit*. It should not be equated with having a constant mood of misery or presenting a long face and an apparently heavy heart. Most certainly we mourn for our sin, but there is also a positive side to all this and it is the comfort of guarding and maintaining our walk with God in joy and serenity of spirit.

The verse quoted at the outset from Psalm 51 – 'The sacrifices of God are a broken spirit: a broken and a contrite heart, O God, Thou wilt not despise' – may seem perhaps to have a formidable sound to it. On examination, however, it reveals much more. It shows that sacrifices can often be made in a formal and indifferent manner when the hearts of believers have little room for God. But there is also another kind of sacrifice when the heart is aware of God's holy character and respects it. This respect virtually keeps us in our right place and produces a tenderness of spirit. There is a vast difference between a crushed heart or spirit and spiritual brokenness. This brokenness has learned to hate those things that come between the believer and God. It causes the believer to sorrow for sin because He loves God and wishes this sweet communion to be preserved. It is this attitude that God will not turn away from, but rather draw near to. There is a longing to safeguard this blessed relationship that sweetens life's pilgrimage even when severely tested. It is a deep desire to be faithful to God, born in the depths of our hearts.

> But ah, this faithless heart of mine!
> The way I know; I know my Guide:
> Forgive me, O my Friend divine,
> That I so often turn aside.   *Alfred Henry Vine*

Without repentance and contrition as necessary activities in our Christian life we would never learn to hate sin and to appreciate that divine companionship of a holy God. Indeed, it is doubtful if we would be teachable at all, because a terrible arrogant attitude can slip in as if we both know it all and have 'arrived' spiritually. We begin to act as if there is nothing more to know, and that suggests in a sense that we think we have reached the limit and exhausted the knowledge of God. Repentance and contrition of heart are a sure safeguard against such an attitude, and they encourage a desire for a deeper and richer experience of God as we learn more of His purity and His ways. We are aware that our relationship with God cannot be broken or even threatened, but the known and felt fellowship with Him can be lost.

> Return, O holy Dove! return,
> Sweet messenger of rest!
> I hate the sins that made Thee mourn,
> And drove Thee from my breast.   *William Cowper*

Sacrifice then takes on a different dimension. The apostle Paul describes true sacrifice and the cost of a transformed life: 'I beseech you therefore, brethren, by the mercies of God, that ye present your bodies a living sacrifice, holy, acceptable unto God, which is your reasonable service' (Romans 12:1). On the basis of the merciful nature of the gospel towards us and our new relationship with God, the apostle is appealing to us to live a totally different style of life. In our physical bodies there must be evidence of a radical change of heart. This calls for a life of determined sacrifice, a life set apart unto God, a holy life that is acceptable in His sight.

The apostle then spells out the implications of such a life: 'And be not conformed to this world: but be ye transformed by the renewing of your mind, that ye may prove what is that good, and acceptable, and perfect, will of God' (Romans 12:2). There is to be a turning away from worldliness: that is, whatever eclipses God from our sight, be it a sin, an unworthy desire, or some inordinate affection. All these things must go, and must not be allowed to intrude again, in order that we may experience a transformed life. It is the evidence of the life of God at work in us and in this way we will know His will in our lives.

To live such a life calls for the exercising of the full force of the words 'repentance' and 'contrition of heart'. This is the sacrifice we make to remain on the gracious altar of His service and to experience the wonder of knowing His will. What a challenge to our modern and casual approach! Or is it modern? Is it not spelt out in the Scriptures for all who would follow the Lord Jesus Christ and walk with God? Our Lord tells us to take up our cross daily and follow Him. This means the cross of our daily obedience to Him in all our circumstances. This is true religion, as described by Joseph Hart:

> True religion's more than notion;
> Something must be known and felt.

Repentance and contrition take us down this godly road. Any light-hearted approach to the Christian faith feels uneasy with such things, and surely will feel uneasy with God, and He with them. It is our solemn and joyful privilege to enter on to this sacrificial way, for our sacrifice is unto Him whose sacrifice for us is above all.

> O for a closer walk with God,
> A calm and heavenly frame,
> A light to shine upon the road
> That leads me to the Lamb!
>
> The dearest idol I have known,
> Whate'er that idol be,
> Help me to tear it from Thy throne,
> And worship only Thee.

So shall my walk be close with God,
Calm and serene my frame;
So purer light shall mark the road
That leads me to the Lamb.   *William Cowper*

6

Faith

*'Now faith is the substance of things hoped for,
the evidence of things not seen'* (Hebrews 11:1).

Faith is high on the list of essentials in every aspect
of the Christian life. The Bible states: 'But without
faith it is impossible to please Him: for he that cometh
to God must believe that He is, and that He is a
rewarder of them that diligently seek Him' (Hebrews
11:6). Such statements make the vital nature of faith
abundantly clear; indeed, there cannot be any realistic personal relationship with anyone without trust.
When trust is lost, all is gone. The crucial importance
of faith in Christianity was shown, for example,
during the time of the Reformation, when faith in all
its spiritual beauty was lifted high before the souls of
men and women, as they found faith in Christ to be
the greatest of all relationships.

We have already thought of the important place of
faith in our salvation. It is also worthwhile to consider
its source, and from that to understand something of
its quality and its influence in our lives.

In the Epistle to the Hebrews there is a very
striking reference to the *origin of faith*. The writer is

describing the Christian life as a race that is to be run with single-mindedness and patience, and with eyes fixed upon the ultimate goal: 'Looking unto Jesus the author and finisher of our faith; who for the joy that was set before Him endured the cross, despising the shame, and is set down at the right hand of God' (Hebrews 12:2). Thus our Lord Jesus Christ is the author, the source and the inspiration of faith. He also sees it through to completion because it comes from Him and belongs to Him.

The apostle Paul describes the essential nature of faith and its source: 'For by grace are ye saved through faith; and that not of yourselves: it is the gift of God' (Ephesians 2:8). Faith is described as God's gift to His people, and that which enables them to embrace the grace of God. Yet this gift of faith is only granted to us in order that we may draw near to Him through His Son. The condition must be that such faith is of an unfailing quality and that it will never disappoint the recipient. God's gifts by their very nature are perfect gifts.

It is this faith that stirs into life in the recesses of the awakened soul and brings it to Christ. It is through this faith that we are able to embrace and be embraced by our Lord Jesus Christ. Faith in Him brings all the benefits of His work for the sinner. Salvation is described as being justified by faith in Christ. In other words, our faith in Christ assures our souls that we are right with God. We are totally accepted because of the life and death of our Saviour, and we begin to learn the profound meaning and worth of all He has done on our behalf. To be accepted by God in this way enables us also to be at peace with God so that we enjoy peace of heart and mind. Toplady, in his hymn describing justification by faith, puts it thus:

> Fountain of never-ceasing grace,
> Thy saints' exhaustless theme,
> Great object of immortal praise,
> Essentially supreme;
> We bless Thee for the glorious fruits
> Thine incarnation gives;
> Thy righteousness which grace imputes,
> And faith alone receives.

The Christian thereafter *lives by faith* and it is this sweet trust in God that makes our walk with Him very real as we become more consciously aware of His work of grace in us in refining our souls. In Hebrews 11 there is an inspiring list of well-known and lesser-known men and women who lived by faith in God. It is a description of faith in action and it shows how faith can be exercised in our daily lives as we trust in God in all our circumstances and believe that we are in His gracious care.

It is a relationship of trust. It would be well nigh impossible to claim that we are never worried or that we are never anxious, but it is possible to be relieved of these heavy burdens. If we are living a life of faith, and if we do trust in God and believe that He cares for us, then we are told to cast all our care upon Him (1 Peter 5:7). It is important to remind ourselves of this when our minds are racing with anxious thoughts,

and our hearts tremble until we are hardly aware of
anyone or anything but our worries. This is the time
to stop and take ourselves in hand and to make all our
concerns known to the Lord. No worry is too great or
too small that He will not hear us and always will
have worked out that which is best for us.

In any case, when we take our concerns to Him,
there is a degree of relief in the act of opening our
hearts to God, and our sense of peace is increased by
our knowledge that we are able to trust our heavenly
Father. We must never forget our relationship: that
the eternal God is our Father and we are His children.
As we have seen already, clear instructions are given
by Paul: 'Be careful for nothing; but in everything by
prayer and supplication with thanksgiving let your
requests be made known to God' (Philippians 4:6). It
is a beautiful invitation and opportunity to tell the
Lord all about our anxieties.

As we do so, we will be reminded in our hearts of
past times when He has guided us through many a
stormy and treacherous difficulty. In remembering
past blessings, our hearts begin to thank Him until we
are full of gratitude to our heavenly Father. We may
ask ourselves what shall we take to the Lord and what
shall we hold back from Him, and the answer allows
no exception. Be careful for nothing! Nothing at all
should be held back. Bring it all with haste to God lest
your joy in Him should be dimmed.

The result of our coming to God and making
known our requests to Him is inspiring: 'And the
peace of God, which passeth all understanding, shall

keep your hearts and minds through Christ Jesus'
(Philippians 4:7). This is a peace that surpasses
anything that can be offered by man. It is a peace that
steadies our hearts, stills the storms and lays hold
upon our minds, clarifying our confusion and enabling us to think *spiritually*. This is the peace that our
Lord speaks about when addressing His disciples:
'Peace I leave with you, my peace I give unto you: not
as the world giveth, give I unto you. Let not your heart
be troubled, neither let it be afraid' (John 14:27).

This close walk with God, or the gracious influence of the life of God in us, is something to be
continually exercised. It is a relationship of trust that
is one of profound comfort, and one which contrib-
utes to the work of grace by driving away fear. In an
awful world there is plenty to cause us to feel afraid.
We fear that our circumstances may change, we fear
the havoc and devastation of war, we fear sudden
sorrow, sickness and poverty. But when faith in God
resides in our hearts, we know that His hand of love
and mercy will never let us go. We face life together
with God. Not only does He think about us but He is
always with His people, and His gentle presence
makes tender our hearts and fills them with gratitude.

With faith in God we are able to face what seem
insurmountable problems and to experience His guid-
ing hand leading us through treacherous circumstances and helping us safely on our way. The example of king Jehoshaphat has always inspired me. Even
though it is an account of the difficulties of a nation,
it was also a personal ordeal for him as king. It was

a fearful time in the history of Judah and it is vividly
described in 2 Chronicles 20. The enemies of Judah
were on the march against the land from every
direction and you can imagine the terrible fear that
gripped the hearts of the people of Judah as the sound
of the trumpets of war and the approaching armies
drew near. All hope seemed to be gone. Then we read,
'And Jehoshaphat feared, and set himself to seek the
LORD, and proclaimed a fast throughout all Judah' (2
Chronicles 20:3). All the people came together and
Jehoshaphat stood before them and prayed. When a
believer prays he does not ever need to panic but
rather to come to God with dignified solemnity, even
though he trembles at his present plight.

Jehoshaphat's prayer is a great one and it begins
in this way: 'O LORD God of our fathers, art not thou
God in heaven? and rulest not thou over all the
kingdoms of the heathen? and in thine hand is there
not power and might, so that none is able to withstand
thee? Art not thou our God, who didst drive out the
inhabitants of this land before thy people Israel, and
gavest it to the seed of Abraham thy friend for ever?'
(2 Chronicles 20:6-7).

King Jehoshaphat goes on in his prayer to describe the sanctuary where God's people gather to
meet with God, especially in times of trouble. He
draws God's attention to the present enemies, whom
God had commanded to be spared in former times.
He points out the ingratitude of these people in their
vicious attack on Judah, which was indeed poor
reward for the kindness shown by God's people in not

destroying them in previous days. He concludes his prayer with a simple and trusting request: 'O our God, wilt thou not judge them? for we have no might against this great company that comest against us; neither know we what to do: but our eyes are upon thee' (2 Chronicles 20:12).

What better direction in which to turn our gaze but to God Himself, because our expectations are from Him? There is a beautiful and touching glimpse of Judah in little family groups waiting on the Lord. The reply came immediately when the Spirit of the Lord came upon one of the Levites and gave him God's assurance of deliverance and victory: 'Hearken ye, all Judah, and ye inhabitants of Jerusalem, and thou king Jehoshaphat, Thus saith the LORD unto you. Be not afraid nor dismayed by reason of this great multitude; for the battle is not yours, but God's' (2 Chronicles 20:15). The transformation is immediate as they change from fear to faith.

Many times in life there seems to be a multitude of problems like a mountain range or an imposing army arrayed against us. Then what should we do? What would God have us to do? What would you do? We turn to God and tell Him all about it and wait upon the Lord. This does not mean complete inactivity or indifference but an active, positive waiting for His merciful intervention in our lives. Living with God, or rather, God living with us and in us, is a relationship of absolute trust. This transforms each day.

A faith that shines more bright and clear
When tempests rage without;

That when in danger knows no fear,
In darkness feels no doubt.   *William Hiley Bathurst*

Faith gives new sight to our eyes as we see things
in a different light. *We see things with the sight of
God*. Fear looks at things and events without God, but
faith never leaves Him out. This changes everything.
When others are in despair and know not where to
turn, the Christian experiences faith shining all the
more brightly and feels the intimate presence of God
even closer. Are you living with Him, and are you
trusting Him, and are you enjoying the pure presence
of God? He loves to see trust in the eyes and hearts of
His children as He pours His lovingkindness upon
them. The greater the difficulty, the firmer His grip
on us. The more fierce the storm, the greater and
warmer is His spiritual embrace around us.

When Peter wrote a letter to Christians who were
suffering bitter persecution, he reminded them of the
One who was keeping them. Amongst the Welsh
Revival people of 1904, there was a familiar reply to
an enquiry about how they were: simply, 'Being
kept'. In short, they were echoing the words of Peter:

> 'Who are kept by the power of God through faith unto
> salvation ready to be revealed in the last time. Wherein
> you greatly rejoice, though now for a season, if need
> be, ye are in heaviness through manifold temptations:
> That the trial of your faith, being much more precious
> than of gold that perisheth, though it be tried with fire,
> might be found unto praise and honour and glory at the
> appearing of Jesus Christ' (1 Peter 1:5-7).

Many years ago I read an illustration on this passage. It described the old method of purifying gold and silver, during which the liquid metal would be heated by fire so that the dross would sink to the bottom of the vessel and remain there as sediment. If under-heated the precious metal would be mixed with impurities, but if it was over-heated then it would be ruined. Apparently, the silversmith or gold-smith would keep a watchful eye on the process until he saw his own face reflected on the surface of the molten metal. He would then remove the vessel from the fire because the metal would be refined and pure. So God refines our faith in Him so that He can see the reflection of Himself in us. Peter goes on to describe the wonder of it all: 'Whom having not seen, ye love; in whom, though now ye see him not, yet believing, ye rejoice with joy unspeakable and full of glory' (1 Peter 1:8).

What a wonderful gift it is to be entrusted with faith, and how great a privilege to place that faith in God! It is a bond that can never be severed. Bathurst's hymn again:

A faith that keeps the narrow way
Till life's last spark is fled,
And with a pure and heavenly ray
Lights up the dying bed.

Lord, give me such a faith as this
And then, whate'er may come,
I taste e'en now the hallowed bliss
Of an eternal home.

One day, faith will complete its work in bringing us safely into the very presence of God. No! Faith does not leave us even then, for it is transformed into sight. There comes a time when we shall live and look on God. What shall we say for such a fellowship, for such loving patience, for such enabling grace? With our souls we shall worship Him.

How good is the God we adore,
Our faithful, unchangeable Friend!
His love is as great as His power,
And knows neither measure nor end!

'Tis Jesus, the First and Last,
Whose Spirit shall guide us safe home;
We'll praise Him for all that is past,
And trust Him for all that's to come.   *Joseph Hart*

7

The Conscience

*'Holding the mystery of the faith
in a pure conscience'* (1 Timothy 3:9).

The conscience is that faculty of the soul which is of
a very sensitive nature. Our immortal souls may be
more fully described as having a centre or hub that is
often called the heart or the spirit. It is here that those
divine actions take place which determine our spiritual direction and our eternal destiny. The soul
expresses itself in five ways, or we could say that it
has five faculties. These are the mind, the memory,
the affections, the conscience and the will. All of us
have these faculties, and although they are governed
by a sinful heart yet they can still show signs to a
greater or lesser degree of what we should be. They
represent a faded remnant of man made in the image
of God. However, in this chapter we will mainly
consider the conscience after God has visited the
heart and when Christ dwells within.

In the *Dictionary of Theology*, conscience is
described by Rehwinkel as that

'faculty in man by which he distinguishes between the
morally right and wrong, which urges him to do that

87

which he recognises to be right and restrains him from doing that which he recognises to be wrong, which passes judgment on his acts and executes that judgment within his soul .... The function of the conscience is threefold. Firstly it is obligatory. It urges man to do that which he regards as right and restrains him from doing that which is wrong. Secondly it is judicial. Conscience passes judgment upon man's decisions and acts. Finally it is executive. Conscience executes its judgment in the heart of man. It condemns his actions when in conflict with his conviction by causing an inward disquietude, distress, shame or remorse. It commends when man has acted in conformity with his convictions.'

In the unregenerate person
Conscience is a kind of guardian or watchman in our souls, and even in the unbeliever there can be considerable activity of conscience. God in His mercy has put some restraint and a measure of favour in human hearts and that is why there are men and women of good conscience who exercise a high moral standard, even though it is inevitably tainted with pride.

At worst, however, it is clear that there can be examples of such brutal and cruel behaviour that it would be easy to conclude that a particular person has no conscience at all. Sadly it would certainly seem so in these ungodly days in which we are living at present. Nevertheless, it would not be correct to assume that such people have no conscience whatsoever. Therefore, it needs to be asked what exactly has happened in such degraded examples. In the Scriptures there is a description of these people: 'Speaking lies in hypocrisy; having their conscience seared with a hot iron' (1 Timothy 4:2). This refers to a kind of spiritual cauterisation caused by constant resistance to the voice of their conscience so that its effect becomes dulled and muffled until it is stifled altogether. Their conscience no longer bothers them and indeed they do not seem to hear its voice at all.

In Christians
There is, however, a very different story when God's grace has visited the heart and all those faculties of the soul are sanctified. The conscience now takes another standard because the measure of judgment is totally changed. In the great work of grace from spiritual death to spiritual life, the conscience in line with the soul has undergone a radical change so that it faces in another direction and is now motivated by God working in us. Together with God's grace, the conscience embarks into another dimension:

'How much more shall the blood of Christ, who through the eternal Spirit offered Himself without spot to God, purge your conscience from dead works to serve the living God?' (Hebrews 9:14).

In the Christian there is a lovely area or ground of appeal where God's Word becomes all important; and as a result, when God is working in us, it is very difficult to silence the voice of conscience.

Even in the experience of the backslider, because

he is a recipient of the grace of God, no matter how deeply he is immersed in the mire of disobedience, he cannot silence his renewed conscience. However far a Christian may wander from God, if he is truly the Lord's, he is never happy. Whatever joys of this sinful world he indulges in, he is left totally miserable. The only way to restored joy is to listen to the voice of conscience and follow its advice to return to the path of obedience.

There are so many benefits in the Christian life but to have a clear conscience is most important in this fulfilment of joy. Our conscience, aided by the grace of God, plays an active part in our growing in grace. We have the responsibility to maintain the balance between God working in us and our own cooperation and spiritual activity. It is our part never to stifle the voice of conscience when it is based on the principles of Scripture. It is essential to keep a clear conscience that guides our actions and does not give cause to grieve the Holy Spirit.

The apostle Paul, writing to the Corinthians, makes a powerful appeal to the Christian's conscience, reminding them that although they have nothing to fear regarding eternal punishment on the Day of Judgment, they are still responsible before the Judgment Seat of Christ. We will be accountable for our use of God's grace after we came to know Him. Our redemption, the salvation of our souls, is assured because of the work of Jesus Christ, both in his obedience to God's law for us and in His payment of the penalty for sin on our behalf. Nevertheless, there will be an assessment of our Christian lives:

> 'For we must all appear before the judgment seat of
> Christ; that everyone may receive the things done in his
> body, according to that he hath done, whether it be
> good or bad. Knowing therefore the terror of the Lord,
> we persuade men; but we are made manifest unto God;
> and I trust also are made manifest in your consciences'
> (2 Corinthians 5:10-11).

This means that we must sharpen rather than dull our consciences in the Christian life or otherwise the thought of the Day of Christ might cause us to be anxious because of the possible shame. To remain morbid and inactive would lead to another rebuke, however many we will have collected – and we will all have collected some. The best remedy, therefore, is to think in a positive manner and to get on with our Christian lives as we live to the glory of God. As we do so, it seems very clear that it is a commendable thing to keep and nurture a good conscience.

Our life with God is a very beautiful experience: to walk in daily communion with Him and to look forward to that wonderful time when we shall be with Him in glory, communing in holiness and love. Every day is sweetened by His unhindered presence when we observe these simple rules. The conscience is that sensitive area where we are most aware of the promptings of God, which cause the conscience to be spurred on to greater heights. With this comes a sense of purity and a life that is without guile. No longer will we allow ulterior motives to govern our behav-

iour, or make that unkind remark that we know will
hurt.

Our Lord described Nathaniel as a man without
guile. To be without guile or duplicity, and to be
governed by a pure motive brings a joy all of its own.
It is to walk heart-to-heart with God, for God Himself
is without guile. No duplicity of any kind can be
found in God: 'Every good gift and every perfect gift
is from above, and cometh down from the Father of
lights, with whom is no variableness, neither shadow
of turning' (James 1:17). If our walk is to be in
harmony with Him, then it must be in such a spirit. A
bad conscience clouds our relationship like a cloudy
sky heralding a gathering storm, but a good conscience keeps a clear sky and the sunshine of His
favour shines upon us.

There is no doubt that a Christian will be tested in
this life and it is sad when unbelievers have room to
criticise. This will happen in any case, but Peter has
something very helpful to tell us:

> 'But sanctify the Lord God in your hearts: and be ready
> always to give an answer to every man that asketh you
> a reason of the hope that is in you with meekness and
> fear: having a good conscience; that, whereas they
> speak evil of you, as of evildoers, they may be ashamed
> that falsely accuse your good conversation in Christ.
> For it is better, if the will of God be so, that ye suffer for
> well doing, than for evil doing' (1 Peter 3:15-17).

It is an excellent thing to have a good conscience and
to live, as far as possible, a life above reproach that is
both harmless and blameless.

We do not look to please men but we are careful that our lives before them are exemplary. We look to please God and are jealous for His glory. The apostle Paul describes the Christian as an earthen vessel through which the light of God shines. His example could be a reference to one of two things and both are applicable.

When the Roman legions returned victorious, bringing trophies and treasures from the palaces of their foes, they would carry them aloft in huge earthen vessels. The vessels were not admired, because they were merely containers for a precious and priceless cargo.

The other reference is that of a very cheap candle holder which had no value of itself but allowed the light to break through the darkness and enabled men to see. Men would not ask for the earthen vessel but they would want to be brought light. We are such earthen vessels and God in us is exceedingly precious, for He is the light and the hope of our salvation.

'For God, who commanded the light to shine out of darkness, hath shined in our hearts, to give the light of the knowledge of the glory of God in the face of Jesus Christ. But we have this treasure in earthen vessels, that the excellency of the power may be of God, and not of us' (2 Corinthians 4:6-7).

His light shines in us in the radiance of His person and as the light of His truth manifests itself in our lives.

When we walk in fellowship with God, a new sensitivity graces our consciences as we partake of the divine nature. There is nothing on earth that can produce this in us; it has to be the very life of God filling and thrilling our souls. This wise little guardian called the conscience is the true conveyer of the heart of God to us. Increasingly, sin becomes more sinful in our sight and, equally, holiness and godliness more wonderful. Who can explain these things? All we can do is tell others about them and show where we found such grace. Godliness in the eyes of the world will always be a mystery, but in a sense it has a mystery of its own to the believer as well. Our duty is to pursue God and to obey Him, 'holding the mystery of the faith in a pure conscience' (1 Timothy 3:9). We must hold on to these things for in doing so we hold on to God and He to us.

> O Jesus, King most wonderful,
> Thou Conqueror renowned,
> Thou sweetness most ineffable,
> In Whom all joys are found!
>
> When once Thou visited the heart,
> Then truth begins to shine;
> Then earthly vanities depart,
> Then kindles love divine.
>
> O Jesus, light of all below,
> Thou fount of life and fire,
> Surpassing all the joys we know,
> And all we can desire:
>
> May every heart confess Thy Name,
> And ever Thee adore;

And, seeking Thee, itself inflame
To seek Thee more and more.

Thee may our tongues ever bless,
Thee may we love alone,
And ever in our lives express
The image of Thine own.

Grant us while here on earth we stay
Thy love to feel and know;
And when from hence we pass away,
To us Thy glory show.   *Edward Caswall*

8

The Mind

'But we have the mind of Christ'
(1 Corinthians 2:16).

The apostle John in his first Epistle describes the Christian life as a life of fellowship with God, in that we walk in the light of God and in His presence. For this fellowship to be meaningful there has to be an openness, an honesty with God, which can perhaps be described as a transparency: 'If we walk in the light, as He is in the light, we have fellowship one with another, and the blood of Jesus Christ His Son cleanseth us from all sin' (1 John 1:7). In this way we ensure that our walk is in true fellowship with our heavenly Father. The mind has an important role to play in this activity.

We may well remember from our schooldays occasions when a diligent teacher in exasperation would say to a child, 'You are able to do this, but you are simply not putting your mind to it.' In the same way it is important for Christians to use their minds. What we think influences our attitudes and the whole of our life. Christians have the mind of Christ and this means that they are in partnership with a very wonderful companion, and that is God Himself. Together with God, the Christian has to think everything through, and look to Him to give the ability to fulfil His desires.

What has Scripture to say about our minds? Although the mind is one of the abilities of the soul or manifestations of the soul's activities, it is very close to the heart or spirit, the hub of the soul. Sometimes, heart and mind seem interchangeable, but it is the condition of the centre of the soul that rules the mind.

In the life of the unconverted person the plight of the mind is a very sorrowful one, spiritually. It makes no difference whether a person has a brilliant mind and sweeps through all examinations with ease, or has only average or very moderate ability. The need for a remedy for a sinful mind remains the same. It is because of the Fall, because of the sin of Adam, because of original sin, that we are in this state. Without exception, all mankind is in this condition and it affects every part of life.

There has to be a change of heart before there is a change of mind, but the mind has an important part to play. Nevertheless it is helpless until the grace of God has visited that heart and replaced the principle of death with that of life, and the principle of sin with that of holiness.

'Wherein in time past ye walked according to the course of this world, according to the prince of the power of the air, the spirit that now worketh in the children of disobedience: among whom also we all had our conversation in times past in the lusts of our flesh,

fulfilling the desires of the flesh and of the mind; and
were by nature the children of wrath, even as others'
(Ephesians 2:2-3).

Such a condition renders the mind incapable of
thinking spiritually, and totally unable to come into
fellowship with God.

The mind can do much, however, in the realm of
embracing a general knowledge of the Christian life
and even adhering to a strict moral code. But it cannot
think or understand the true nature of the Christian
faith until that wonderful time when God visits the
heart and the mind is enlightened. It does not suddenly become a brilliant mind that is capable of
solving great mathematical or scientific problems. It
does not change in that way, but something has
happened that enables the mind to think clearly about
eternal issues. This enlightenment transforms everything.

The first object of delight and beauty that presents
itself to the mind is our Lord and Saviour Jesus
Christ. From now onwards the soul can claim that it
has the mind of Christ, and it can think spiritually.
This miracle is described in so many ways in the
epistles, including a change from being aliens, stran-
gers, enemies and foreigners to being heirs of God,
co-heirs with Christ, the citizens of heaven. It is small
wonder that the mind has undergone a radical change.

Of course all our troubles are not over, because the
mind has been in the rut of sin for the whole of our
lives and has become long accustomed to thinking in
that manner. However, there is now a ground of

appeal since the mind has a new ability which needs to be encouraged and exercised. This is important because the mind has a vital part to play in our spiritual progression. It is the mind that feeds the emotions with thoughts which cause distress or joy. It is the mind that presents to the will a course of action to be followed. There can be only one direction and that is heavenwards, only one destination and that is God Himself.

How are we to deal with unworthy and uncharitable thoughts that come to the mind? How shall we tackle these persistent distractions, that often come to us when we are endeavouring to read the Scriptures and to pray? It seems at those times particularly that our minds are diverted and our thoughts wander far away.

Sometimes it is due to the evil suggestions of Satan coming near to the frontiers of the mind, or because our own unworthy desires are still lurking, ready to rise to the surface. In a moment of weakness, when we are off our guard, such thoughts can rush to our minds and gain entry. Afterwards we feel badly about this and feel very sorry that we have allowed our minds to indulge in this way so that our thoughts are drawn away from God. Scripture is quick to give us the advice we need to follow on such occasions, and we find it works effectively:

'For the weapons of our warfare are not carnal, but mighty through God to the pulling down of strongholds; casting down imaginations, and every high thing that exalteth itself against the knowledge of God,

and bringing into captivity every thought to the obedience of Christ' (2 Corinthians 10:4-5).

In this way we will find a progression taking place in
our Christian lives. Our minds must be active in our
Christian walk; we are to be alert and to keep a watch
over our souls.

In Paul's first prayer in his Epistle to the Ephesians (1:18), he prays that believers may advance in
wisdom and knowledge:

> 'the eyes of your understanding being enlightened;
> that ye may know what is the hope of His calling, and
> what the riches of the glory of His inheritance in the
> saints.'

There has to be that initial touch of God upon the soul,
but afterwards there is a progressive enlightenment
as our minds embrace more and more of His truth. All
this calls for determination to be finished with all
those things to do with spiritual darkness, and to
pursue God. As we work it out day by day, God is with
us giving us enabling grace. The mind is no longer
trapped in sin but is able to cooperate with God and
to prove something of what it means to have the mind
of Christ.

When Paul wrote to the Romans he made a powerful appeal in the twelfth chapter to those who have
known the mercies of God in salvation and found
peace in Him:

'I beseech you therefore, brethren, by the mercies of
God, that ye present your bodies a living sacrifice,
holy, acceptable unto God, which is your reasonable
service. And be not conformed to this world: but be ye
transformed by the renewing of your mind, that ye may
prove what is that good, and acceptable, and perfect,
will of God' (Romans 12:1-2).

The appeal is to be willing to live a sacrificial life, a
godly life, a life that has literally been transformed.
The secret of it all is the renewing of the mind as God
takes control and daily strengthens and renews it for
the task in hand. As a result we will be able to respond
to such an appeal.

Satan's clear aim is to keep us in his grip and to
prevent us from exercising this clarity of mind with
spiritual understanding. 2 Corinthians 4:4 refers to
him blinding the minds of unbelievers so that they are
deprived of the light of the glorious gospel. But for
the Christian, Satan can no longer blind our eyes
because God has given grace so that sight comes to
our sightless eyes. However, Satan can certainly
throw a great deal of dust into our eyes by distracting
us with some old besetting sin. We must determine to
keep a clear mind, for we know that with such a
resolve God will never fail us.

The quality of the thoughts of our minds will be
exalted as we consider more and more the person of
Christ. Paul, in writing to the Philippians, urged
them, 'Let this mind be in you, which was also in
Christ Jesus' (2:5). He then describes the suffering of
our Lord Jesus Christ as His willingness to submit

Himself to such a death on our behalf; thus although we realise that the sacrifice on Calvary was a penalty for our sin, yet it also provides a perfect example of submission to His Father's will, and total obedience to the plan of God and the ordeal that faced Him. It is our part to be like-minded in obedience to God and to be willing, and with a good spirit to serve Him gladly, even when it means sacrifice.

If anxiety should press upon us and cause our hearts to be heavy and our minds to be in a turmoil, we must go to the Lord, for He invites us to share our concerns with Him and cast all our cares upon Him. There are such times when we find it difficult to concentrate on spiritual matters or to pray. It is not because of sin or some foolish distraction but due to a general sense of anxiety. Even so, we are able to call for help and there is guidance on how we should go about it. The Lord reassures us in His Word, 'Be careful for nothing' (Philippians 4:6). Let nothing disturb your peace or take away your joy.

But if the heaviness persists, then make it known unto God, the One who never leaves you or forsakes you. When at last we come to God with our request for assistance, He comes to our aid, and the promise is a very blest one: 'And the peace of God, which passeth all understanding, shall keep your hearts and minds through Christ Jesus' (Philippians 4:7). What a promise! The safe-keeping of God is ours at such times, just as if He were taking over full control of the helm.

His first word to us is 'peace' for He knows we need to be at peace, and the quality of the peace He gives passes all understanding. It is the same peace that our Lord spoke about when He said that it was not the kind of frail and temporary peace that the world gives. His peace quietens the storm in the heart and stills the panic of the mind. It is the peace of God as He works out His purpose in us.

> What a Friend we have in Jesus,
> All our sins and griefs to bear!
> What a privilege to carry
> Everything to God in prayer!
> O what peace we often forfeit,
> O what needless pain we bear,
> All because we do not carry
> Everything to God in prayer!
>
> *Joseph Medlicott Scriven*

The guidelines in the Bible on how our thoughts should be directed are quite clear, because our minds wander so easily from the things of God:

'Whatsoever things are true, whatsoever things are honest, whatsoever things are just, whatsoever things are pure, whatsoever things are lovely, whatsoever things are of good report; if there be any virtue, and if there be any praise, think on these things' (Philippians 4:8).

Instead of dishonesty in our minds, it is to be replaced by honesty. Instead of injustice and a censorious spirit, we must be fair and just in our thinking. Instead of impure ideas and motives, which have such a powerful driving force, they are to be replaced by a pure heart and mind, leaving no room for evil thoughts to lurk. Instead of the ugly features of life where mankind distorts or destroys all that is good, there must be the beauty of Christ.

To rejoice in that which is good, virtuous and praiseworthy is a wholesome outlook and it is a privilege which Christians have received from our Lord Himself, as we learn from His followers such as Paul and others down through the ages. The reward is a truly great one: 'And the God of peace shall be with you' (Philippians 4:9). There can be no greater comfort than to have a mind at peace and to enjoy the fellowship of the God of peace in our lives.

> May the mind of Christ my Saviour
> Live in me from day to day,
> By His love and power controlling
> All I do and say.
>
> May the Word of God dwell richly
> In my heart from hour to hour,
> So that all may see I triumph
> Only through His power.
>
> May the peace of God my Father
> Rule my life in everything,
> That I may be calm to comfort
> Sick and sorrowing.
>
> May the love of Jesus fill me
> As the waters fill the sea;
> Him exalting, self abasing,
> This is victory.

May I run the race before me,
Strong and brave to face the foe,
Looking only unto Jesus
As I onward go.

May His beauty rest upon me
As I seek the lost to win,
And may they forget the channel,
Seeing only Him.   *Katie Barclay Wilkinson*

9

The Will

*'Wherefore be ye not unwise, but understanding
what the will of the Lord is'* (Ephesians 5:17).

Whenever we come to a decision it is an act of our
will, and it can be described as the climax of a process
in which the will acts as a servant of the soul. What
I mean is that the mind has considered a matter, and
probably the feelings are also involved if it is something of any consequence, then the will is engaged in
that final decision. We often describe a person as
being strong or weak willed: that is, someone who is
either easily influenced or who is stubborn or un-
yielding. Most of us are somewhere in between these
two extremes.

The will is that faculty that takes a course of
action, and once the decision has been made, it is
irreversible. Sometimes such a decision is good and
sets a person on the right course in life, but at other
times it is the very opposite and causes endless
heartache and sorrow for many people.

The will in sinful people

In the ordinary, natural man the will is a servant or an expression of a sinful heart. It is governed by the gratification of self and angered by anyone or anything that frustrates its purposes. We can take for example a child with its winsome ways but unless it is directed rightly, that same lovely child becomes wilful and spoilt. In effect the will soon manifests the influences of original sin. It is the same story for every individual as they seek to have their own way, cost what it may in regard to the wellbeing of others. It is a similar pattern amongst the nations of the world, because the will of man is governed by a fallen nature that will manifest itself eventually on a small or a large scale.

Consider the game of bowls, in which each bowl is weighted or biased. The idea is to roll the bowls along the green so that they stop as near as possible to a small white ball. However, the problem is that, because of the weight on one side, each bowl follows a curved path, so the players have to try to take this into consideration. Sometimes the bowl curves hopelessly wide of the mark. On other occasions it will make a straight run that seems to have overcome the weight, and then suddenly there is a twist in its course as it turns to one side. Sooner or later the bias shows.

It is the same with our behaviour, for at some time or another our prejudice in favour of sin will make itself evident and we miss the mark, lamentably so. Countless times we make promises to improve our ways, but always end in failure. Why should this be

so? It is because a sinful heart will always want to be
gratified.

The will of the Lord Jesus
There is an example in the Scriptures of someone
who was very different. The Lord Jesus Christ set His
face toward Jerusalem, fully aware of its implications. Although He was the Son of God, yet on earth
He put Himself under the will of the Father and
delighted in obedience: 'For I came down from
heaven, not to do Mine own will, but the will of Him
that sent me' (John 6:38). It is when we come to the
Garden of Gethsemane and that awful yet wonderful
act of sacrifice that was to take place on Calvary when
He died for our sins, that we see His gracious submission to the eternal plan and glorious will of God.

The scene is extremely moving, when all heaven
must have held its breath as the great redemptive act
of Calvary began. He had withdrawn to the garden to
pray where He uttered these striking words: 'Father,
if Thou be willing, remove this cup from Me: nevertheless not My will, but Thine, be done' (Luke
22:42). It would be impossible for us to enter into His
experience in Gethsemane, but we are given certain
indications of what He went through.

No doubt, a vivid picture of what was about to take
place was in His mind as He thought of Isaiah's
description of the Messiah being wounded and bruised,
and having our iniquities laid on Him: 'He was
wounded for our transgressions, He was bruised for

our iniquities: the chastisement of our peace was upon Him; and with His stripes we are healed' (Isaiah 53:5). No doubt, He would also be acutely conscious of being forsaken as He recalled the words of Psalm 22:1: 'My God, My God, why hast Thou forsaken Me?' As well as this, all Satan's hosts would have assaulted Him with particular hatred at that time. His entire human nature would recoil in horror at the contents of the cup before Him. Nevertheless, we see divine and absolute obedience to the will of God as He accepted that He had to follow the way of the Cross of Calvary.

We find the same theme in Philippians 2:8: 'And being found in fashion as a man, He humbled Himself, and became obedient unto death, even the death of the cross.' Such obedience surpasses our thoughts and imaginations, and from this act of submission of His will to the will of God, we follow Him to Calvary and see the result of that obedience. Justice is satisfied. Hell is vanquished. Sinners are pardoned.

The will in the Christian

When a child is wilful it needs to be guided and directed, but not crushed. It is not God's will to crush His children until they have no expression of their own. This could hardly be His intention.

Do you recall those Wild West scenes when the cowboy hero would ride an untamed horse? The incredible energy of the horse in all its frantic and powerful antics has thrown off many a rider previously, but this time it has met its master. The hero remains calmly seated in the saddle and triumphantly guides the horse around the arena. Is the horse now useless? It was before, because its energy was wasted in wild and uncontrolled behaviour. Now, however, the tamed horse is still full of energy and can take its master untiringly on long journeys as if horse and rider had almost become one.

Similarly, the rebellious will meets its master in Christ, who now controls and guides its vast energies into the ways of grace. Not crushed, but sanctified, it is forever learning the Master's will.

To continue the illustration: it is obvious that once it has been tamed, the horse needs to be shown much patience as it is taught new ways. In the case of show-jumping, for example, what endless patience and perseverance must be exercised by the trainer! Master and animal have to get to know each other well, before the horse begins to show results in responding to the rider's praise and being willing to serve him.

The illustration has a point, but the will is not a horse. This human will of ours has long been used to having its own way and does not take easily to another authority over it. Even when the sinner has come in submissive faith to Christ, and mind, affections and will have all displayed the desire of the heart to trust in the Saviour, there is still so much to be learned regarding the will of God in our lives. The hidden rebellion of our stubborn will can still raise its proud head even in a child of God.

The story of grace is a fascinating one, for God is

the author and He does quietly and firmly cause that story to be a triumph of His grace as well. He is forever teaching us. Sometimes when we are particularly difficult and unwilling to follow His path, finding it too costly or too sacrificial, He still has His way in bringing us round to accept His will.

Chastisement

It is the natural desire of all parents to see their sons and daughters grow into fine young people. It is because we love them that we have this desire, and at times it will be a costly love when we have to correct them. A good parent would never do this out of malice or in anger, or from a desire to harm or hurt their child. Is it not so with us since God desires us to be more than conquerors? He desires that we should both glorify Him and enjoy Him.

> 'My son, despise not thou the chastening of the Lord, nor faint when thou art rebuked of Him: for whom the Lord loveth He chasteneth, and scourgeth every son whom He receiveth. If ye endure chastening, God dealeth with you as with sons' (Hebrews 12:5-7).

How terrible it is to hear parents say that they are giving up on their child. It means they no longer care what the child does or what trouble it gets into because they have washed their hands of the child. How much more dreadful it would be if God should give up on us! What a fearful prospect! What utter desolation! Indeed, such a thought makes His rebukes become sweet as they are an assurance to our immortal souls that He is treating us as His own, and has not and will not give up in His dealings with us.

However good our parents and teachers may be, their patience can be exhausted, but God's patience is never exhausted. His purposes will be fulfilled, no matter how strange the way may seem at times. We are often blinded by things because we stand too near to them. I once taught art, so let me give an illustration regarding painting.

Suppose that you have been busy painting for hours and are very gratified inwardly with your efforts, although of course you would not say so. You feel that it looks good – indeed, very good. Then you stand back a few yards and see some glaring examples of wrong shades and other faults, but you are still largely satisfied. You then leave the painting on one side for a time, and when you take a fresh look it is obvious that much work needs to be done to put it right. So too our Christian lives are lived in the midst of circumstances that affect our decisions, but God sees the whole picture and quietly guides our reluctant wills, and it is only later, in this life or the next, that we are grateful for His infinite wisdom and patience with us.

Let me continue with another example from my experience in art. I well recall returning home with some of my own paintings at the end of a college term when I was in training. I was anxious to have my father's opinion of them because he was a very fine artist. He looked at them carefully for a while, then quietly took a brush and palette and added touches here and there. The pictures became alive! He kindly said to me, 'When will you learn the value of shadows, of light and shade?' Of course, he was so right. We do not like shadows in our lives, but they do something to make us more tender and sensitive.

We must not be afraid of the will of God, because it is working in a detailed way which is best for us. We must trust His perfect will.

> Ye fearful saints, fresh courage take;
> The clouds ye so much dread
> Are big with mercy, and shall break
> In blessings on your head.

How well that expresses our experience! Often we are fearful; we forget past mercies; our memories are incredibly short. We forget the times when we were in the shadows and how they matured and mellowed our nature.

> Judge not the Lord by feeble sense,
> But trust Him for His grace;
> Behind a frowning providence
> He hides a smiling face.

We must always remember that the sunshine of His grace never leaves us. God loves us and knows what is the very best for us at all times.

> His purposes will ripen fast,
> Unfolding every hour;

> The bud may have a bitter taste,
> But sweet will be the flower.
>
> Blind unbelief is sure to err,
> And scan His work in vain;
> God is His own interpreter
> And He will make it plain.   *William Cowper*

As the years go by and our fellowship with the Lord deepens, we become the readier to accept His will and to understand His profound wisdom. We could not imagine life without Him. He fills our thoughts as He fills our days. When we surrender our will to Him, it is not a matter of losing all individual initiative, but rather of receiving a new ability through a will refreshed, renewed and remade. We are then able to make spiritual decisions. Paul loved his blessed imprisonment which made him free to love God and live to His glory.

> Make me a captive, Lord,
> And then I shall be free;
> Force me to render up my sword,
> And I shall conqueror be.
> I sink in life's alarms
> When by myself I stand;
> Imprison me within Thine arms,
> And strong shall be my hand.
>
> My heart is weak and poor
> Until it master find;
> It has no spring of action sure,
> It varies with the wind:

It cannot freely move
Till Thou hast wrought its chain;
Enslave it with Thy matchless love,
And deathless it shall reign.

My will is not my own
Till Thou hast made it Thine;
If it would reach the monarch's throne
It must its crown resign:
It only stands unbent,
Amid the clashing strife,
When on Thy bosom it has leant,
And found in Thee its life.   *George Matheson*

10

Forgiveness

'Forgiving one another, even as God for Christ's sake hath forgiven you' (Ephesians 4:32).

One of the most striking descriptions of a Christian is found in 2 Corinthians 5:17: 'Therefore if any man be in Christ, he is a new creature: old things are passed away; behold, all things are become new.' At first reading this is a very encouraging and a very beautiful verse, and so it is. On reflection, however, the implications are startling and far reaching because it means that a total and a radical change of lifestyle has to take place. The old ways have to go and a new life emerges. Men and women have fought hard throughout the centuries to find a formula that will embrace both the old, sinful lifestyle and the new, or at least include a certain percentage of the former. Never more than today has this tedious battle been evident, when the very gospel itself is being accommodated to allow professors to live according to the ways of sin.

But Paul's statement contains a principle which is much more basic, and that is that we are in Christ and all the spiritual benefits that this implies are available to us now, as well as glory to come. The effect of this is that we are virtually new creations; we have en-

tered another realm, another life, and most certainly
and happily we have another direction and destination. If we claim to be Christians then we must accept
the reality of the life of God in us. Our Saviour came
that we might have this life in abundance (John
10:10).

One of the most sensitive and delicate issues to be
considered in this new life is the subject of forgiveness. When we have been deeply wounded or un-
justly treated to the point of feeling terribly damaged,
it becomes a very hard challenge to forgive the
offence from the depths of one's heart. It is a matter
that applies to us all at some time or another because
it is unavoidable that situations will arise which face
us with the demands of forgiveness. It is a question
that affects nations as well as individuals, but for
Christians there can be no compromising answer. If
God's people clash over some issue and turn their
backs on one another, then to restore the fellowship
and friendship they once enjoyed presents a searching challenge.

The example of Jesus

Let us begin by looking at the Saviour and at the very
heart of His mission here on earth, when during His
crucifixion He utters those unforgettable words to
those around Him, 'Father, forgive them; for they
know not what they do' (Luke 23:34). In His agony,
and as He faced that great penalty for sin in our place
when the wrath of God for sin was poured upon Him,

He yet had the heart and mind to forgive His abusers. From a human point of view He had every right to call for destruction upon the treachery of the religious leaders, the fickleness of the crowd and the weakness of His own disciples, but He did not. Something of the same spirit of forgiveness is reflected in the martyrdom of Stephen when he asked, 'Lord, lay not this sin to their charge' (Acts 7:60).

If we believed that this was all there was to Christ's death on the Cross, then that alone would be most inspiring to our souls, but we know that there is a far deeper meaning to the Cross which reaches to the heart of this issue of forgiveness. It is something which cannot be passed by because it is fundamental to everything involved in being a Christian.

The cost of forgiveness

Man's greatest need is to be right with God. As a result of the sin of Adam, and what is termed original sin which has permeated and influenced every human being ever since, man's fellowship with God is broken. Our abilities and achievements are many and, as we are told in the Scriptures, we are fearfully and wonderfully made (Psalm 139:14), yet all that we do, even our very best, is tarnished with some form of sin which affects the baser and finer points of our nature alike: 'For all have sinned, and come short of the glory of God' (Romans 3:23).

Evidence of this abounds in the story of mankind both individually and collectively, indeed we have

only to consider the events of our enlightened twen-
tieth century! Mercifully and gloriously we have the
devising of God's plan for the rescue of fallen mankind.

In order that fellowship might exist between God
and ourselves, something had to be done for us. All
our efforts, however sincere, are doomed to miserable failure, for God knows our helplessly sinful
hearts. This great miracle is achieved by God's
matchless grace and His divine plan. The Lord Jesus
Christ, the second Person of the Trinity, co-equal
with the Father, takes on board a human nature, albeit
perfect. In the person of Christ is this mystery of two
natures which was essential for the task in view.

One of the ways that men and women use to try
and avoid this offence is to make light of the righteousness of God but to make themselves appear more
righteous than they can ever hope to be. This was the
method used by the Pharisee in the temple when he
paraded all his wonderful achievements before God
in his boastful prayer (Luke 18:11-12). However, we
are clearly told that our salvation is 'not of works lest
any man should boast' (Ephesians 2:9).

What then did the Lord Jesus Christ do for us? The
sinless Saviour, although tempted by Satan, was
victorious in all His answers and responses. He put
Himself under the law of which He was the author.
He had nothing to prove by doing so because He was
pure and holy. He did it in order to fulfil the requirements of God in our place, namely that we should
love God and our neighbours with our whole being.

He then took upon Himself our failure to keep that law, and on the Cross He faced the punishment and wrath of God instead of us: 'And the Lord hath laid on Him the iniquity of us all' (Isaiah 53:6).

Something of the depth of this can be gained from the words of our Lord on the Cross, 'My God, my God, why hast Thou forsaken Me?' (Mark 15:34). In quoting these opening words of Psalm 22 the Lord knew the reason for His suffering. It was because God's holiness could not tolerate sin, but we with our puny minds can hardly begin to grasp the meaning of the absolute purity of God's holiness. Sin cannot be ignored or passed by, because it offends against such holiness.

The experience of the Saviour on the Cross is so profound that our best expositions fall far short. The wrath of God against sin is met in its full force by Him, and He does this for us so that we do not have to bear the penalty for our sin. Three days later there was the physical resurrection when God vindicated, approved, and made known His acceptance of His Son's sacrifice for sin. We must always bear in mind that this is God's plan and that Christ laid down His life for our sakes: 'Who was delivered for our offences, and was raised again for our justification' (Romans 4:25).

The awakened soul cries out in concern at the very thought of such love:

> Eternal Light! Eternal Light!
> How pure the soul must be,
> When, placed within Thy searching sight,

>   It shrinks not, but with calm delight
>   Can live and look on Thee.   *Thomas Binney*

To the convicted soul it seems impossible that it
could ever possess that calm delight before God and
still survive in His presence for, as Binney wrote:

>   O how shall I, whose native sphere
>   Is dark, whose mind is dim,
>   Before the Ineffable appear
>   And on my naked spirit bear
>   The uncreated beam?

The hymn goes on to tell the story of grace and the
way of salvation:

>   There is a way for man to rise
>   To that sublime abode:
>   An offering and a sacrifice,
>   A Holy Spirit's energies,
>   An Advocate with God.

Then follows the experience of repentance and that
gift of faith, both of which are now awakened into
activity through the preaching of the gospel, until we
come to the result of it all:

>   These, these prepare us for the sight
>   Of holiness above;
>   The sons of ignorance and night
>   Can dwell in the Eternal Light
>   Through the Eternal Love.

A forgiven soul, dressed in the purity of Christ, and who is at peace with God and right in His sight, now faces the progression in this new life. This in no way contradicts his position in Christ, which is due entirely to faith in Him and the embracing of these glorious gospel truths. We are forgiven completely and, in the words of another Toplady hymn, 'Debtors to mercy alone'.

The position of the Christian is indeed a happy one in this costly and tender relationship with God through the Saviour. He is able to say: 'In Whom we have redemption through His blood, the forgiveness of sins, according to the riches of His grace' (Ephesians 1:7). When we face up to the reality that we are a forgiven people the question then arises: what kind of people should we now be in our relationships with others? Should we show some reflection of Stephen's example when he was stoned for his faith? The reason why Stephen forgave was because he himself was a forgiven sinner. That is the secret we ourselves must seek to learn.

Forgiving others

Our Lord gave an example of this in one of His parables. It concerns a man who owed his lord 1,000 talents, but who could not repay this vast sum. His lord was angry with him and would have taken severe measures were it not that he responded to the pleas for mercy by this man on behalf of his family and himself. The lord therefore forgave him all the debt.

Later, however, this same greatly forgiven man had a servant who owed 100 pence, and despite the plea for time to pay by this poor servant, the man's heart was not moved and he took cruel action to demand repayment in full from him. Everyone was shocked, especially the lord when he heard that the man who had been forgiven so much had showed no mercy over such a pittance. His pitiless attitude rightly provoked the anger of the lord who ordered that the man should be fully punished (Matthew 18:23-35).

The main point of this parable was that the foolish man had not understood the nature of forgiveness. But have we learned that lesson? If we have, do we then exercise this grace? Paul encourages those who have been forgiven so much to show this generous spirit: 'And be ye kind one to another, tenderhearted, forgiving one another, even as God for Christ's sake hath forgiven you' (Ephesians 4:32).

Prior to relating the parable the Saviour had been speaking to His disciples about the topic of forgiveness and had laid down certain principles for them to follow. The principles make spiritual sense to us all if we have the heart to obey them. The kind of forgiveness that merely states 'forget it' can still fester in our hearts and from such a careless attitude no true fellowship can ever be restored. This can sometimes border on sentimentality while still bearing a grudge in the heart. An offence is an offence!

It is important to take note of the Lord's words concerning this matter:

> 'Moreover if thy brother shall trespass against thee, go
> and tell him his fault between thee and him alone: if he
> shall hear thee, thou hast gained thy brother' (Matthew
> 18:15).

To trespass causes offensive behaviour in every way
that we can imagine, so there are no exceptions
allowed. However, what happens if the one who
causes offence has not the grace to receive you or ask
forgiveness? Jesus continued:

> 'But if he will not hear thee, then take with thee one or
> two more, that in the mouth of two or three witnesses
> every word may be established. And if he shall neglect
> to hear them, tell it unto the church: but if he neglect to
> hear the church, let him be unto thee as an heathen man
> and a publican' (Matthew 18:16-17).

At that point the disciple Peter posed the question:
'Lord, how oft shall my brother sin against me, and
I forgive him? Till seven times?' No doubt Peter felt
he was being most generous in suggesting a fair offer
which showed a gracious spirit.

However, the Lord replied: 'I say not unto thee,
Until seven times: but Until seventy times seven'
(Matthew 18:21-22). Jesus then related the parable of
the merciful, forgiving lord and the cruel, unforgiving servant. It was a startling illustration of the
principle He wanted to emphasise: namely, that the
forgiven person's heart must be right.

In the parallel passage in Luke 17, our Lord points
out the harsh and judgmental attitude of the Pharisees

and how wrong they were. It is inevitable that offences should come in such a world as this, but how easy it is to be so wrong in our attitude in correcting others, thereby causing great hurt to these ordinary and vulnerable people. The disciple must show a very different spirit. Whilst rebuking the offender, he is to leave the door wide open for repentance and acceptance. The point our Lord is making is that there are to be no hindrances or limitations to our forgiveness: we must forgive the repentant every time. There is no such thing allowed as saying, 'That was your last chance, enough is enough!' To this he gives an emphatic No. Always forgive the penitent.

Luke 17:3-4 states: 'If thy brother trespass against thee, rebuke him; and if he repent, forgive him. And if he trespass against thee seven times in a day, and seven times in a day turn again to thee saying, I repent: thou shalt forgive him.' This brings a practical, robust attitude into such a situation. Whilst the offence is not glossed over but exposed, yet the repentant is freely forgiven always. However, our Lord's word regarding failure to exercise this spirit of forgiveness is one of severe rebuke (verse 2): 'It were better for him that a millstone were hanged about his neck, and he cast into the sea, than that he should offend one of these little ones.' We must not harbour a judgmental and unforgiving spirit, but have a heart that is ever ready to forgive the repentant.

There is really no escaping this matter of a genuine forgiving heart. Indeed, if we are careless and neglectful in this matter we fail to recognise the very

nature of the gospel. Are we not forgiven sinners, first
and foremost? Take, for example, the Lord s Supper,
where we are remembering particularly our Lord's
sacrificial death for our sin. From any point of view,
can it be right to approach His table while harbouring
a grudge against a fellow Christian, or dwelling in our
minds on uncharitable thoughts? It would be a fundamental contradiction. It is essential in as far as in us
lies to have made time to be at peace with one another
in preparation for such a spiritually sensitive service.

In another example our Lord gives a clear injunc-
tion on a related area of forgiveness.

> 'But I say unto you, That whosoever is angry with his
> brother without a cause shall be in danger of judgment:
> and whosoever shall say to his brother, Raca, shall be
> in danger of the council: but whosoever shall say, Thou
> fool, shall be in danger of hell fire. Therefore if thou
> bring thy gift to the altar, and there rememberest that
> thy brother hath ought against thee; Leave there thy gift
> before the altar, and go thy way; first be reconciled to
> thy brother, and then come and offer thy gift. Agree
> with thine adversary quickly, whiles thou art in the way
> with him; lest at any time the adversary deliver thee to
> the judge, and the judge deliver thee to the officer, and
> thou be cast into prison' (Matthew 5:22-25).

From this it is quite clear that the Christian must be
both without offence to his brother and prepared,
when offended, to put matters right with his brother.
Effective action is advocated in both cases. The one
who is the cause of the offence has a duty to make
peace with his brother.

Our Lord shows that there are three stages: personally, with a witness, and before the church. Having done these things his responsibility in that sense is over. Likewise, for the offended party there must be, as in the case of the relevant parable, a readiness to forgive the offender when it is evident that there is sorrow and repentance for the offending act. This pattern is practical and consistent with God's requirements.

However, there is a further aspect that must be considered since we have to understand what makes it possible to forgive or to seek forgiveness. It is essentially a matter of the heart, in either case, whether a Christian is well received or not. It is possible that the one who has caused offence and who wishes to be at peace may be rejected, or the one who has been offended finds that the offending party seems totally indifferent and shows little change of attitude. It is at such times that we must ensure that our hearts are right. No opportunity should be allowed for a root of bitterness to take hold, and if it does, we are told to pluck it out (Ephesians 4:31).

When we examine the problem of causing and taking offence, it seems in the end to be a matter of 'self'. The remnants of the influence of our old man on our sensibilities linger on and allow hurt, anger and bitterness to fester. We can always justify our behaviour in one way or another so that we can hide behind a screen of some kind of righteousness.

> This cruel self, Oh, how it strives
> And works within my breast,

> To come between Thee and my soul
> And keep me back from rest.   *Handley Moule*

We must come to that place where we have thought this through spiritually. The obstacle of being offended or causing offence can be a terrible stumbling block to our walk with God. Spiritually speaking we cannot look the other person in the eye as we seek to justify ourselves. Usually we blame everyone and everything except ourselves, but our spirit of animosity will show itself in all sorts of ways. Then how can we be right in this matter?

We must face up to ourselves and be honest with God. The Psalmist said:

'Search me, O God, and know my heart: try me, and know my thoughts: and see if there be any wicked way in me, and lead me in the way everlasting' (Psalm 139:23-24).

When we stand before God, a new realisation of how much we have been, are and, indeed, will be forgiven comes over us, and surely we will also have a sense of gratitude. If we have appreciated something of the cost of our salvation and that the sinless Saviour took all our uncleanness and meanness upon Himself and died for us, then how can we remain unmoved, unaffected and unchanged? In the light of this we should consider our brother or sister and realise that we both can and will take the right steps. A heart melted by the grace of God is a new and tender heart and there is no room for malice in that heart.

But are we able to do this on our own – that is, to forgive or even to be forgiven, and to have a tender heart and a desire to restore fellowship? No-one would dispute that this is a costly thing. There is a vast difference between this and a superficial cover that never deals with the sin. The latter can never be thought of as true fellowship but rather it is a fraudulent act to display our generosity of spirit that costs absolutely nothing, and often fails to recognise the offensiveness of sin. The true change of heart is a delicate and sensitive procedure. It is a genuine desire to put God first in our lives, so that the quality of our forgiveness and of our submission might display the power of God's grace in us. In a sense we have no right any more to indulge in our bitter or angry feelings: 'For ye are bought with a price: therefore glorify God in your body, and in your spirit, which are God's' (1 Corinthians 6:20). Christ died for us that we who live should not henceforth live unto ourselves, but unto Him who died for us (2 Corinthians 5:15).

Nevertheless we need help to be on our guard or else these powerful selfish attitudes can return, especially if the offence re-occurs. If we are determined to be men and women of grace and do not wish anything to ruin our fellowship with God and with each other, then this area must be carefully protected. When writing to the Philippians, Paul gave some excellent guidelines: '... work out your own salvation with fear and trembling' (the implications of salvation in our lives, which would be our sanctification),

'for it is God which worketh in you both to will and
to do of His good pleasure' (2:12-13).

There has to be this willingness as a Christian to
think through these Scriptural principles, and doing
so will be of immeasurable value to the wellbeing of
our souls. The remarkable grace of God operates
therefore by enabling our will and our ability to carry
out this act of obedience. The glory is to God, since
it is His life that is in us, yet there is also that balance
of human responsibility where we are involved and
are held accountable by God.

The result of this in our daily living is enrichment
as the loveliness of His grace fills our souls, our cup
overflows and we have genuine joy. We have gained
a brother or we are received as a brother. What better
result? What happier way can there be than the way
of grace? Although costly, that is swallowed up in the
joy of doing our Father's will.

11

Temptation

'Resist the devil, and he will flee from you'
(James 4:7).

It does not take Satan long before he makes his presence known to the Christian. Since he is unwilling that any soul should come to Christ, Satan opposes God and hates every activity of the gospel and the work of God's grace in the hearts of men and women.

Our Lord, speaking to His disciples when seventy of them had returned from a mission preaching about the Kingdom of God, told them concerning Satan, 'I beheld Satan as lightning fall from heaven' (Luke 10:18). This was a reference to the occasion when God cast this high-ranking angel out of heaven.

Although powerful, Satan is not all-powerful. He has an individual personality and a cunning mind, and whereas God alone knows the thoughts of our hearts, Satan has a pretty good idea of our weaknesses and strengths. In 2 Corinthians 2:11, Paul gives a general warning which is a robust and practical directive in this realm: 'Lest Satan should get an advantage of us: for we are not ignorant of his devices.'

131

The methods that Satan and his evil angels exercise are many. In the area of deception he is able to appear plausible in his arguments and his appeal. Paul tells us: 'And no marvel; for Satan himself is transformed into an angel of light. Therefore it is no great thing if his ministers also be transformed as the ministers of righteousness' (2 Corinthians 11:14-15). This shows how he will enter the area of religion and of spirituality and deceive a soul. Our Lord Jesus Christ warns of false teachers who dress up as sheep but inwardly are ravening wolves, and would tear at our souls and bring dismay to our spiritual lives.

As well as this, Satan will look for those vulnerable areas of our lives to take advantage of us: 'Be sober, be vigilant; because your adversary the devil, as a roaring lion, walketh about, seeking whom he may devour' (1 Peter 5:8). Satan is always on the prowl seeking opportunities, most especially when we are off our guard. It is true that he will attack those parts of our lives which are weak and most vulnerable. Yet I remember a wise and godly minister giving me contrasting advice on this matter. He believed that most Christians would be especially careful to guard their weaker points, but added that they seldom give thought to those areas where they are strong and feel sure of themselves. These are the areas we often leave unguarded and through them Satan can easily take the shine from our Christian life by making us proud and self-confident.

The devil never wearies. He is always ready to whisper some temptation, some deception or some

note of despair into our minds – right up to our
deathbeds. But, and it is a glorious 'but', the apostle
John in his warning against seducing spirits and
servants of Satan says: 'Ye are of God, little children,
and have overcome them: because greater is He that
is in you, than he that is in the world' (1 John 4:4).

It is therefore vital to know our own position. Let
it be abundantly clear that the Christian, that person
who is born again and whose sins are forgiven, can
never be lost. Once established in the grace of God,
we are there for eternity: 'My sheep hear my voice,
and I know them, and they follow me: and I give unto
them eternal life; and they shall never perish, neither
shall any man pluck them out of My hand' (John
10:27-28). Nevertheless it behoves us to be cautious
and careful when such an enemy of souls is about, for
though he cannot cause us to be lost, he is able to bring
us into distress and sorrow.

There is, therefore, a spiritual battle in which we
are sure to be involved in one way or another. There
are some things that were perhaps in our lives previously which, although attractive, were wrong, and we
must flee from them or else we become easy prey. We
are also able by God's grace to remain steadfast in the
faith and stand against the devil's evil intentions.
Though our preoccupation must be with God and the
blessed gospel of our Lord and Saviour Jesus Christ,
we must needs be on constant guard against the
approaches of Satan to the frontiers of our minds,
intent on trying to get his foot in the door.

Then what shall we do? We must walk with the

Lord and keep close to Him in sweet fellowship. But
what are the things which we must guard in order to
maintain our walk with God?

Christian priorities

Let us begin with *prayer*, which includes communion
with God. We need to remember that we are in sacred
communication with our glorious God. There is
private prayer during those times that we set apart to
come to the throne of grace and bring everything to
Him. However great or small our concerns and requests may be, we must make them known to our
Lord: 'Let us therefore come boldly unto the throne
of grace, that we may obtain mercy, and find grace to
help in time of need' (Hebrews 4:16).

During our daily lives, although we give our most
diligent attention to the task in hand and serve our
masters well, there is a sense in which we are always
near to God and our hearts are inclined towards Him.
We are able at all times to appeal to Him from our
hearts if we are troubled, because the fellowship with
Him is unbroken even in the midst of our busy lives.
We are to pray without ceasing (1 Thessalonians
5:17).

Prayer in the Christian's life is closely linked with
the reading of the Scriptures. We know that these
writings are of immeasurable worth and contain all
that we need to know for our salvation and sanctification. They are inspired, infallible and inerrant: 'All
Scripture is given by inspiration of God, and is

profitable for doctrine, for reproof, for correction, for instruction in righteousness: that the man of God may be perfect, throughly furnished unto all good works' (2 Timothy 3:16-17).

There is an important place for devotional study in the life of every Christian. As we read a portion of Scripture each day, probably during our prayer time, the Lord speaks to our hearts, sometimes in rebuke but often in comfort. We also need to study the Bible with the aid of a reliable written commentary on the Word of God, so that we are greatly enriched by knowing the background to what we are reading.

But in addition to our prayer time and the reading of the Scriptures there is something else. The Church has prayer meetings where God's people come together to pray, and meetings around the Word of God where together we are pastorally led in the study of the Bible.

There is also the matter of *Christian fellowship*. When we become Christians we do not forsake our old friends and acquaintances, unless it means that we remain in bad and sinful company where we could easily be dragged down. Clearly that would be wrong, but although we do not neglect former friends, we will also make new Christian friends and with them we are able to have not only friendship, but fellowship as well as we share the experiences of the Lord in our lives.

All these things we must cherish and maintain because Satan will try to distract us in any way he can in order to spoil our Christian fellowship. We need this relationship and walk with God, and we need fellowship with each other. Guard these things well.

The Lord's Day

Are we not told in Scripture to honour God's Person, His Name, and His Day? Some would claim that they can worship God in nature. There is an element of truth in this since we are able to agree with George Wade Robinson:

> Something lives in every hue
> Christless eyes have never seen.

But we are part of His Church on earth and we submit to being 'fitly framed together' (Ephesians 2:21). The worship of God on the Lord's Day is enriching to our souls and a powerful witness. Because such activity is clearly revealed in Scripture we know that it is right, however costly or difficult it may be. It is an occasion for looking at Christ and not at one another, except in love and desiring each other's good.

> 'And let us consider one another to provoke unto love and to good works: not forsaking the assembling of ourselves together, as the manner of some is; but exhorting one another: and so much the more, as ye see the day approaching' (Hebrews 10:24- 25).

Here again, Satan would use all his wiles to convince us of how tired or misunderstood or busy we are on the Lord's Day. We need to encourage and support each other, and even if we say that we need no one, then that claim can be dismissed because others may need us. It is both our duty and our privilege to keep the Lord's Day and to worship God together. In the keeping of this devotional part of our lives, we will be strengthened because we know that it is well-pleasing to God and that it maintains our fellowship with Him as we do this together. It is worth remembering that in heaven this fellowship with Him and with each other will be for ever.

Spiritual Armour

When Paul wrote to the Ephesian church, a church that later is described in the Book of Revelation as having lost its first love, he goes into some considerable detail regarding this spiritual battle. The main command is *to make a stand*:

> 'Finally, my brethren, be strong in the Lord, and in the power of His might. Put on the whole armour of God, that ye may be able to stand against the wiles of the devil. For we wrestle not against flesh and blood, but against principalities, against powers, against the rulers of the darkness of this world, against spiritual wickedness in high places. Wherefore take unto you the whole armour of God, that ye may be able to withstand in the evil day, and having done all, to stand' (Ephesians 6:10-13).

The apostle gives the picture of a battleground where the forces and powers of Satan are arrayed ready to attack. On our side there is the might and strength of God. Nevertheless we have to withstand the wiles of Satan and, after the onslaught, to *stand* by the grace of God. Paul advises that we can only do this if we wear the whole armour of God.

Paul uses the battle dress of a Roman soldier as an example, and each part of the armour is significant. He begins with the main article of clothing needed in the stand against Satan's powers: that is, the loin cloth or garment, which he associates with *truth*. I suggest a two-fold explanation for this: namely, truth itself as described in the gospel and the teachings of Scripture; yet also it could include the result of applying this, which is a quality of integrity in the truthfulness of the believer. It implies the very opposite of a liar, especially since the Lord describes Satan as the father of lies.

To protect the heart and lungs, those precious life-giving parts of the body, a breastplate was necessary. Spiritually this is the breastplate of *righteousness*, that is, the position of the Christian in Christ, whereby sin and unrighteousness have been taken away and the punishment for them paid on the Cross of Christ. The Christian now wears that righteousness of Christ which is accounted for him, or imputed to him. At the same time the result of this is godliness of life which leaves no room to doubt the integrity of the believer. This is called imparted righteousness, as the life of Christ is imparted to him and growth in grace becomes increasingly apparent.

When Satan tempts me to despair,
And tells me of the guilt within,
Upward I look, and see Him there
Who made an end of all my sin.

Because the sinless Saviour died,
My sinful soul is counted free;
For God the Just is satisfied
To look on Him, and pardon me.
Charitie Lees De Chenez

For the soldier, his footwear was very important because an enemy would often scatter sharp pieces of metal on the ground to render opponents helpless. Just as it is important how we live, it is also important where we go. Our feet are to wear the preparation of the gospel of *peace*. Of course this means that we bear the tidings of the gospel that brings peace with God to men and women, but it also means that we are peacemakers, so that whoever we visit will benefit from our company as we leave the savour of Christ behind us.

In addition, we need to remember the shield of *faith* to protect ourselves from Satan's fiery darts as he harasses us with doubts and fears. It is vital that the shield must always be in position to stop these darts in flight or else they can inflict serious damage. Faith, in the Christian, is justifying faith whereby he has availed himself of the pardoning grace of God in our Lord Jesus Christ. This faith is meant to be used actively in our lives in all the varied situations that we face.

O for a faith that will not shrink,
Though pressed by many a foe;
That will not tremble on the brink
Of poverty or woe.   *William Hiley Bathurst*

We must not be careless regarding the mind for
we are told to wear the helmet of *salvation* by which
the head is well protected. How important it is to
guard our thoughts and to think on those things
described as 'lovely' by Paul. Primarily our thoughts
are fixed on our safe and sure salvation, but our busy
minds can so easily be occupied by the cares of this
world. To the Philippians (4:8), Paul wrote:

> 'Finally, brethren, whatsoever things are true, whatso-
> ever things are honest, whatsoever things are just,
> whatsoever things are pure, whatsoever things are
> lovely, whatsoever things are of good report; if there be
> any virtue, and if there be any praise, think on these
> things.'

Thus far the pieces of the armour have been for
our defence and protection, but now we come to the
sword. We are told that the sword of the Spirit is the
Word of God, and that we are able to take it and to use
it. This Word is all we need, in the power of the Holy
Spirit, and in battle we declare its contents to men and
women. Despite Satan's efforts to undermine the
truth, we do not lay this sword down. It is either in use
or kept ready at our side. Our Lord answered Satan by
the Word of God, and it is ours also for every
eventuality.

'For the Word of God is quick, and powerful, and sharper than any two-edged sword, piercing even to the dividing asunder of soul and spirit, and of the joints and marrow, and is a discerner of the thoughts and intents of the heart' (Hebrews 4:12).

Remember that Satan is a defeated foe, his days are numbered and his power is limited. His is not the final victory, so let us be careful that he does not gain little, temporary victories that frustrate and hinder the work of grace for a while. Never take Satan lightly, but take God seriously and let us avail ourselves of His vast resources to overcome the enemy of our souls.

> And were this world all devils o'er,
> And watching to devour us,
> We lay it not to heart so sore;
> Not they can overpower us.
> And let the prince of ill
> Look grim as e'er he will,
> He harms us not a whit:
> For why? his doom is writ;
> A word shall quickly slay him.
>
> *Martin Luther, tr. by Thomas Carlyle*

12

Love

'This is my commandment, That ye love one another, as I have loved you' (John 15:12).

We live in a world that is dominated by greed and hatred, and where endless warring factions mercilessly harass each other for some territorial or monetary gain. It has been the story of human life throughout the centuries as the earth cries out with the voices of multitudes of people who have suffered. The same cut-throat incentive has been the driving force behind big business, occasionally masked with some small gift to a charitable institution.

What is it in mankind that makes us so vicious and self-centred? The answer is sin, and the malaise lies deep in the heart of man. Nevertheless the world is certainly not devoid of any virtue. There is the love shown in friendship which can reach great heights of self-sacrifice for another person, or even for a nation when a loyal allegiance has a motive that is commendable. It would be wrong to say that there is no good in mankind, yet even at its best there is always that subtle self-love that will intrude somehow and spoil it all.

The Christian is a new creature in Christ and is capable by God's grace of achieving greater heights as a person than he could ever have hoped for on his own. He is able to love, and to do so with a new ability that draws upon resources and reserves that were not available to him before. This love is divine in origin and its quality cannot be found outside the Christian experience. We need to consider how this is possible and how this is exercised.

It is to God Himself that we must look for the answer. When we consider the being of God as we are instructed in Scripture, we recognise that out of all the great attributes He possesses, there are those which can never be fully communicated to man – such as omnipotence and omnipresence – while there are other characteristics and qualities, though perfect in every way, which are communicable to us in some degree.

God's holiness and love

One quality stands out as His crown, and that is His holiness. It is indeed the crowning beauty of the character of God. It is this attribute that sets God apart and makes Him so distinctively different to our-selves. We are sinful and He is holy. This theme runs through the Bible and is depicted in Revelation 4:6 by that vast area of sparkling white diamond that sur-rounds the throne, representing the holy character of God.

Holy, holy, holy! all the saints adore Thee,
Casting down their golden crowns around the glassy sea;
Cherubim and seraphim falling down before Thee,
Who wert, and art, and evermore shalt be.
Holy, holy, holy! though the darkness hide Thee,
Though the eye of sinful man Thy glory may not see,
Only Thou art holy, there is none beside Thee
Perfect in power, in love, and purity.

Reginald Heber

In order to have fellowship with God we too must be holy.

In the heart of God a way has been devised so that a sinner may approach and be accepted by Him for eternal fellowship. This plan is motivated by love, that divine love which brought together in the Godhead a remarkable way for the eternal benefit of man and for the glory of God. It was a triune scheme whereby a holy God could receive sinners into fellowship with Himself. How could this be done without compromising His holiness? Sin could not be overlooked or passed by unpunished. In His love God provides a means by which this can be achieved.

The way of love
Let us consider God expressing His character in the Ten Commandments. These commandments could be described as a law of love in that they require a perfect love towards God and a perfect love towards our fellow human beings. That is, we are to honour God's Person, His Name and His Day and, in respect

of our fellows, not to murder, steal, lie, covet, and so on. This shows a quality of love that has content to it and is not just a vague or sentimental feeling.

The problem lies in our inability to rise up to these expectations. It is here that we see God's love in action. He provides the means. Our Lord Jesus Christ was willing to submit to the law of God in our place and fulfil it for us, then to take upon Himself our deserved punishment at Calvary. Consequently, through repentance for our sins and faith in the Lord Jesus Christ, we are forgiven and are at peace with God.

> 'In this was manifested the love of God toward us, because that God sent His only begotten Son into the world, that we might live through Him. Herein is love, not that we loved God, but that He loved us, and sent His Son to be the propitiation for our sins' (1 John 4:9-10).

Now this being so it follows, by the very nature of God's love expressed to us in His Son, that we should respond, and there can only be one response to such love: 'Beloved, if God so loved us, we ought also to love one another' (1 John 4:11). Not only are we confronted with this glorious attribute, but the love must also be in us.

Indeed, if it is not present in us it strongly implies a contradiction and casts doubt upon the integrity of our experience of God. It poses the question whether we ever had been recipients of His love, since there must be evidence of it in our lives. Note how clearly John expresses this:

'We love Him, because He first loved us. If a man say,
I love God, and hateth his brother, he is a liar: for he that
loveth not his brother whom he hath seen, how can he
love God whom he hath not seen? And this commandment have we from him, That he who loveth God love
his brother also' (1 John 4:19-21).

It is inconceivable that a Christian should be
lacking in love when he himself has been the recipient of such love which has acquired eternal security
for him. Nevertheless, if the life of God is to be
manifested in the believer so that love flows through
his very veins, there is a responsibility upon the
believer to actively exercise this love. The old ways
die hard; old grievances and prejudices and old
offences that should have been long forgotten are
easily rekindled. It is particularly at such times that
we need to exercise a love that is superior to our own.
Human love at its best can reach a breaking point but
divine love knows no limits.

To exercise this love and to cooperate with God's
grace is our privilege and our duty. Without this love
our profession becomes very empty, but with this
love our lives and the lives we touch are enriched
immeasurably.

The walk of love
It is important to remember that Christians are ordinary people and that we are subject to the same
frustrations, disappointments and hurts as all people
are. As Paul stated at Lystra, 'We also are men of like

passions' (Acts 14:15). While therefore there is a great potential of love in the believer, there must also be that willingness to draw on these vast spiritual resources of love that we have in God. Sadly we often do not avail ourselves of this love and can so easily allow anger or some unkind attitude to manifest itself and thus let a root of bitterness take hold. The fact that we are children of God does not mean that love will always be our automatic response. To exercise the life of God in ours we must give our willing co-operation.

In the days of the early Church, which were often times of bitter persecution when many Christians were martyred, a comment was made respecting their love towards one another. However hard we may be tested, the love of God should be apparent in our lives. I am not suggesting that this is an easy exercise, especially when our patience is severely tried. The only way to do this is to be aware of God's love to us in Christ and to remember God's many acts of lovingkindness and tender mercies on life's journey.

When we begin to think in this realistic way it does put the present situation into its correct perspective and helps us to exercise love. As well as this, we call on the Lord to enable us and to grant us the required grace. In all this we are learning to walk with God so that His love might be more and more evident in our lives.

1 Corinthians 13

The quality and the calibre of such love is described in the well-known thirteenth chapter of 1 Corinthians.

Love is stated to be the greatest of gifts, but the lack of love has frightening implications. Whatever spiritual gifts I may exercise and boast, if I am lacking in love, then I am nothing. Nothing! The very sound of the word echoes with despair. Such a thought forces us to jump to attention and recognise that love is a vital feature of the being of God and the life of the believer. No gift we possess, no sacrifice we make is comparable to love.

Love is then described as suffering long and being kind. There is no trace of envy or of vanity in love. Love bears itself well and is not self-seeking. It is determined not to be provoked or distracted, and neither thinks nor dwells on evil. Love, that is the love of God, finds no delight in sin but rejoices in God's truth and also in truthfulness. Love is willing to forbear and to believe trustingly. It shines with hope and, for the sake of the Lord, it is willing to endure all opposition. Other things may fail, others cease to have their use, but love will never fail or fade or cease to have its place. It is by grace alone and total dependence upon God that such love may be exercised and practised in our lives.

The Lord Jesus Christ commanded His disciples to follow this commandment of love, and in John's first letter it is the measuring rod which shows whether we are the Lord's or not.

What does this call for?

Our wish should be that God's life and love might be evident in our total demeanour in order that this might glorify God. It certainly beautifies the Christian character and, as we live our lives or perform our daily duties, we are observed and our lives are like an open letter for many to read. Who knows how far such a life will reach, or what sorrow it will touch and comfort? Love is so beautiful a feature in the Christian life that it simply is not worth allowing anything to spoil it or hinder its effect. Love is of God. Let us not forget that in such a sad and sinful world, love is like a lamp of grace that makes the Christian's life invaluable and above price amongst the people with whom he is in contact. It is well worth our most determined effort to pursue God so that His love might be in us.

Losing love

Although we usually associate the apostle John with love, the same urgent emphasis was often struck by Paul in his writings. We have only to think of that chapter on love in 1 Corinthians which we considered earlier, to realise the importance he placed on the matter. Also, in his Epistle to the Ephesians, Paul's second prayer (3:14-21) deals with the topic of love and its necessity in the life of a believer. It may well be that Paul was giving some indication of a lack of love in that church, because in Revelation 2:4-5 this failing is fully exposed and condemned:

'Nevertheless I have somewhat against thee, because thou hast left thy first love. Remember therefore from whence thou art fallen, and repent, and do the first works; or else I will come unto thee quickly, and will remove thy candlestick out of his place, except thou repent.'

What had happened amongst the Ephesian Christians? They were involved in the sin of the Nicolaitans. Whatever can that be? It is the problem that has dogged the Church throughout its long history: that is, the Christians there had come to some arrangement with the ways of the world, little realising that the world is greedy for the love of our hearts and will share it with no-one, least of all with God.

There is no way possible to share our love with any other love when we are the Lord's. I realise that this view can easily be misconstrued. Therefore, let me hasten to add that those who love God with all their hearts will love their family and friends better than the person who puts even the best of people first in his heart.

Love encouraged

Paul prays for the Ephesian believers that they might be strengthened in the inner man so that they can contain this love:

'That Christ may dwell in your hearts by faith; that ye, being rooted and grounded in love, may be able to comprehend with all saints what is the breadth, and length, and depth, and height; and to know the love of Christ, which passeth knowledge, that ye might be filled with all the fulness of God' (Ephesians 3:17-19).

As we have seen in an earlier chapter, Charles Simeon called this prayer 'the celestial ladder', and small wonder because it leads to the fulness of God. What an expanse of spiritual beauty and glory! Not only does the love come from God, but all the strength and willpower comes from God also.

It is no wonder that we are encouraged to exercise this gift of love towards God and man, for as believers we have the grace to achieve it. It is the life of God in His people. This is the hallmark of our discipleship.

What will this cost us? The price is high. It will cost the love of self and that passionate protectiveness of our own interests. It calls for enormous determination and spiritual discipline. But we have the example of Christ to encourage us.

The path our Saviour trod to Calvary was a path of love. How can that be so when He was in the midst of such cruel hatred, hypocrisy and even desertion by His friends? It was because He loved His Father and His Father's will. The way of the Cross is often referred to as the way of sorrow and misery, but that is not the complete picture. Ahead of Him Jesus saw a multitude washed in His blood, their sins gone forever, and dressed in His righteousness. It was love that motivated God to send our Lord into this world. It was love, a passionate and perfect love, that led Him to the Cross.

My own background and early ministry were entirely in the Welsh language. Later I was called to serve the Lord in a large city and to minister in English. I was unfamiliar with the Scriptures in English and my knowledge of English hymns was very limited. On my first Sunday I chose to close the morning worship with a very lovely hymn:

> It is a thing most wonderful,
> Almost too wonderful to be,
> That God's own Son should come from heaven,
> And die to save a child like me.

As I announced the hymn I suddenly realised it was included in the section of the hymn book entitled 'Hymns for Children'. I can still remember to this day how hot and embarrassed I felt as I blushed a deep scarlet. But today how do I feel? What a hymn! What words! And what inspiration led the writer to pen such thoughts! It is a hymn for all, since we are all children under age in this world and we are forever learning.

> I cannot tell how He could love
> A child so weak and full of sin;
> His love must be most wonderful
> If He could die my love to win.
>
> *William Walsham How*

I wonder if He has won our love? I pray that He has. If love settled our great debt then how many other problems and troubles can be faced and over-

come by love? By God's grace we can walk this way,
so that His love may be richly shed abroad in our
hearts – a strong love, an undaunted love, a coura-
geous love, a victorious love: the love and life of God
in us.

13

Death

' ... a time to die' (Ecclesiastes 3:2)

I once heard a man praying most earnestly regarding
his future spiritual condition as he considered his
own advancing years and the remorseless march of
time. He was still comfortably in his forties and his
prayer was that God might make him godly in his old
age. Although his words rang with sincerity there
seemed to be no particular urgency about the matter,
until he paused for a moment. Then he corrected
himself and asked that the Lord might begin the work
of godliness in his life immediately. I realised that the
implication of what he was asking had relevance in
many aspects of our lives because our good intentions are of little value if they are continually post-
poned to some far distant time. For example, the wise
student keeps a steady pace all the year around, whilst
many others only settle down to work when they see
the examinations looming over the horizon.

Sooner or later there comes a time when every
person has to bid farewell to this life and face the
inevitable and unavoidable fact of death. All that we
are familiar with and which seemed to go on for ever

will come to an end when death almost rudely inter-
rupts our life, and we take the first steps from the
reality of things known into another realm and dimension altogether.

Everyone is bound to think about this at some time
because there is no way that we can escape the
knowledge of death. It confronts us in the world
around, and when members of our family and close
friends and acquaintances have gone. It looms large
in our thoughts, no matter how dismissive we may be.

No doubt some will say that our end will merely
be as a candlelight extinguished, but they are still left
with that doubt in their minds that there may be an
after-life, and even a Creator – God. Some will dull
their minds with the pleasures of the moment or fill
their lives with busy activities to distract them from
considering their end. Others will cling to a vain hope
that God would not and indeed could not reject them.

But whatever the surface arguments or the ready
flow of words that are advanced, the problem remains unsolved and they feel unsure and perturbed.
One of my grandsons, who was aged three at the time,
felt very keenly the death of his other grandfather.
While being prepared for bed one evening he looked
at his mother and said, 'You won't grow old, will you,
Mam?' She asked him why he was so concerned and
his simple, yet thoughtful, reply was, 'Well, old people
die, and they don't come back.' He had understood
the reality and finality of death very well. Many
people live as if they go on for ever, not realising that
death is a respecter of neither persons nor age.

The reason why the introduction of this subject has been stated so bluntly is because of its importance. I do not want to suggest for one moment that we should be morbidly preoccupied about the matter to the extent that our lives become over-shadowed with a constant gloom. Even so, because death is inescapable, to be unprepared for it is sheer folly. J.C. Ryle stated that even for a Christian believer who is leaning upon the Lord with the assurance of God's promises, death is a solemn experience, for he has never been this way before – but for the unbeliever it is unthinkable.

> There is an hour when I must part
> With all I hold most dear;
> And life with its best hopes will then
> As nothingness appear.   *Andrew Reed*

How should a Christian think about death? The fact that a person has received the Lord Jesus Christ as Saviour does not mean they should pay no heed to that moment. The Christian faith sheds a clear light on the whole matter, starting with the basic teaching that our souls are immortal and incapable of dying. It is true that there was a time in the past when we did not exist, but there never will be a time in the future when we shall not exist.

Verses such as 'This night thy soul shall be required of thee' (Luke 12:20) bring a new dimension to the whole matter and cause a number of questions to spring to mind. Where does the soul go? Will it meet with God? What will He have to say, especially about me?

It is so convenient to believe in the annihilation of the soul, for it is an easy, even pleasant option. Nevertheless it is an erroneous teaching and it does not change the fact that the unconverted soul will be in the horror of utter despair as it pathetically faces God and His judgment and eternity. It is indeed a sorrowful thing to be ill-prepared for that final and decisive moment when the soul appears before God Himself. Consider well these matters, oh dear soul!

The Christian faith whispers hope to believers and tells them of 'an inheritance incorruptible, and undefiled, and that fadeth not away, reserved in heaven for you' (1 Peter 1:4). We have the words of our Lord when He told His disciples that His task was to go ahead, in reality via Calvary, and prepare a place for believers where He would be and where they would join Him.

He described heaven in those unforgettable words that have comforted and assured millions of people of the loveliness of their destiny: 'In my Father's house are many mansions: if it were not so, I would have told you' (John 14:2). What a statement! It tells us so much in so few words. Heaven is more palatial than all the palaces of earth multiplied together. Heaven is home, as implied by the simple phrase, 'In my Father's house'. Surely this also suggests that it is homely. But that is not all. He rests this promise on the integrity of His person and His character by stating, 'If it were not so I would have told you.' This is consistent with the God that cannot lie and in whom there is no duplicity.

The source of comfort

Introducing these glimpses of heaven in John 14, the Lord Jesus Christ speaks these comforting words, 'Let not your heart be troubled.' So often we feel troubled, particularly when we consider how little we have achieved. How frequently we have left our promises dangling for some future date! How we wish that we could have done more for a loved one, even when we feel that we did all our strength allowed! How we wish that many a thoughtless act, an irritable word that was meant to hurt, an uncharitable thought that stormed in our minds could all be eliminated as if they had never happened!

Yes, we are often troubled by such things, and sometimes the concern is the thought of the valley of death that lies ahead of us. What will my entry be like? Will He come without warning and without notice to tap my shoulder and bid me home? We may regret that we left so many expressions of gratitude unsaid, so much left undecided and undone.

Possibly we will be granted adequate time and warning and have to face the struggle of a body striving to live against some final illness. How will I bear such a time? Will I maintain my witness? Will I lose my joy? Will I question His wisdom or His timing? His simple answer to all this is, 'Let not your heart be troubled,' and He adds this assurance, 'Peace I leave with you, My peace I give unto you: not as the world giveth, give I unto you. Let not your heart be troubled, neither let it be afraid' (John 14:27).

Fear of Death

It must not be forgotten or discounted that we are
creatures of emotion. Once we are Christians we do
not cease to feel, and this should always be taken into
account. Facing death is an awesome thing. I am not
ignoring the comfort, peace and strength that are available to us, the anticipation of glory and the presence
of God. Not at all; but the fact remains that we have
never been this way before – we have not died before.
If Satan persists in tempting us during our life he
certainly will not give up at our end. Fear is real, and
can raise its ugly head: in fleeting times of apprehension, wondering what the end will be like and whether
I will let my Lord down. Fear has many guises.

I can think of a few instances where a steadfast
soul has had a moment like this and I have had the
privilege of pointing them to a little word frequently
overlooked in a great verse: 'For so an entrance shall
be ministered unto you *abundantly* into the everlasting kingdom of our Lord and Saviour Jesus Christ' (2
Peter 1:11). I have often delighted in the abundant
entrance and the glorious welcome awaiting the
Christian.

As well as this I have also delighted in describing
the kingdom of our Lord. However, it is in speaking
to the dying that I have learnt the true value of that
word 'ministered'. What a word! Just as nurses help
a helpless patient from the bed to a chair, so we shall
be ministered to and carried and ushered home. We
are not left stranded, like a child in a new school
leaning on the school wall at playtime desperately

wanting a friend. No, we are expected and we are
cared for in every respect. In Psalm 23 we are told that
we are not alone: 'Yea, though I walk through the
valley of the shadow of death, I will fear no evil: for
Thou art with me; Thy rod and Thy staff they comfort
me.'

I saw a new vision of Jesus,
A view I'd not seen here before,
Beholding in glory so wondrous
With beauty I had to adore.
I stood on the shores of my weakness,
And gazed at the brink of such fear;
'Twas then that I saw Him in newness,
Regarding Him fair and so dear.

My Saviour will never forsake me,
Unveiling His merciful face,
His presence and promise almighty,
Redeeming His loved ones by grace.
In shades of the valley's dark terror,
Where hell and its horror hold sway,
My Jesus will reach out in power,
And save me by His only way.

For yonder a light shines eternal,
Which spreads through the valley of gloom;
Lord Jesus, resplendent and regal,
Drives fear far away from the tomb.
Our God is the end of journey,
His pleasant and glorious domain;
For there are the children of mercy,
Who praise Him for Calvary s pain.

William Vernon Higham

Preparation is essential

A well known youth organisation has the commendable motto, 'Be Prepared'. It may not have been
meant in any spiritual sense, but rather in a practical
and sensible way to be ready and equipped for all the
sudden problems of life. The same words may be
given a deeper meaning, which is to be prepared for
eternity.

The first essential for the Christian *is to be sure of
his position in Christ*. We are told to examine ourselves to see if we are in the faith or not (2 Corinthians
13:5). This certainly does not mean developing a
morbid introspection or a state of endless pre-occu-
pation with self-examination. However it is good to
consider the redemptive, the saving work of the Lord
Jesus Christ in us.

I know deep in my heart that He lived a life for me
that I could never live, and died a death for me that I
would otherwise be dying eternally. We must never
lose sight of the fact that our spiritual rebirth and our
total dependency rest upon Him. This will help us to
appreciate that all this was decided in eternity before
the foundation of the world, when we became the
recipients of such mercy that will always overwhelm
our understanding and cause us to stand humbly in
His sight. Yet we should never lose the sense that we
are much more than forgiven sinners. There must be
no contradiction between what we believe and how
we behave, they must be held together in a knot of
grace.

Ready to die

Some years ago a young man from Germany appeared in our church prayer meeting. He was on an exchange visit organised at that time by the teaching profession. He attended all the means of grace and loved the meetings of the congregation, so that he soon won a warm place in our hearts. Then the Christmas vacation came and he went home to his parents. I well remember opening some cards that arrived one morning and there was one from Germany. I naturally assumed it was from Siegfried but I was puzzled over the words and I decided to take it with me to the prayer meeting that evening to get it translated by someone who knew German. However, there was something about the card which at first I regarded as a possible cultural custom in Germany. Why was it in black print surrounded by a thick black border? Then I noticed what appeared to be two dates, and it occurred to me that Siegfried's father had died, until I realised that the dates gave an age of twenty-three. Shortly afterwards his father contacted me and I learned the details of Siegfried's death. He had been returning home from a church meeting when a drunken driver had struck his autocycle and he had been killed. His father requested that I should go to his flat to sort out his possessions and send anything of importance home to Germany.

It was one of those experiences that a person would prefer not to have, and certainly not a task anyone would seek to do. However, I went to the flat and I was not surprised to find everything exceed-

ingly neat and tidy. Even his letters were in orderly
bundles with elastic bands and name labels on each
one. There was nothing that would cast any kind of
doubt in my mind and all I can say is that he was well
prepared. The verse that came to me was, 'Remember now thy Creator in the days of thy youth' (Ecclesiastes 12:1). This he had clearly done for there was
nothing hidden in his life; it was indeed a transparent
walk. What is the message of this? Surely it is that a
Christian of any age should always be prepared and
live each day to the glory of God, ready at any time
for His homecall.

This instance is only one of many I could mention,
but it serves to remind us that the remaining years of
anyone's life may not be all that numerous. Indeed
we have to accept that we reach a point when the
years we have had are far more than those to come.
The Scottish saying, 'Thatch your roof in fine
weather,' is good advice in the spiritual realm, for
when the heart, soul and mind are in glorious unity
and harmony with the Lord Jesus Christ, then life will
contain few regrets.

Dying well
I believe that there are those occasions when God
heals and restores, and we are given an extension to
our days, as was granted to King Hezekiah (2 Kings
20). It is with profound reverence and respect that I
say that I do not doubt the ability of the Lord to heal,
although such examples are comparatively rare.

However, there are other times when, pray as we may and plead as we will for a dear relative or friend, restoration does not take place. The question I am often asked as a minister of the gospel is, 'How can I face this prospect with dignity and grace?' Hopefully the following account will provide the answer.

Late one evening after a particularly sad and discouraging day when I had utterly failed to help the person I had visited, I returned home to find a message beside the telephone asking me to go to a certain home for the elderly. I hastily made my way across the city to the home, which cared for about twenty people, one of whom I knew well. She was over ninety years old and had been a radiant Christian since the day the Lord drew her to Himself.

The matron gladly received me and showed me to a room where I found the elderly believer sitting bolt upright in her bed with a shawl over her shoulders, looking for all the world like a queen in her own right. She had suffered a very minor stroke and, although the effects were hardly perceptible, she sincerely believed that a major stroke was to follow. I took her hand and asked if she had something to tell me. 'Yes,' she answered quietly, 'Before long, perhaps in the next few hours or days, I shall be going home.' She then proceeded to tell me what fine, even religious people her companions in the home were. Nevertheless she feared that none of them had a saving experience of the grace of God and she felt herself to be a person of no influence, just another old lady coming to the end of a very long road. Then came her request: 'Tell me, Pastor, for the sake of those around me, how shall I die well?'

My reply was a simple one. I told her to die as she had lived. She would be merely stepping from our little day into God's lovely day. She would close her eyes here and open them in glory. The dear soul smiled contentedly and, to the glory of God, that is exactly what happened. But what a beautiful request! She had wanted to maintain a faithful walk to the very end, and had been granted grace to do so.

Let us think about our own approach to the time when the ties of earth must be severed and we put our hand in His and enter the everlasting kingdom of our God.

Anticipating our departure can be illustrated in this way. Imagine your doctor calling to see you during an illness and sitting by your bedside calmly and without any urgency to go on to his next patient. With great care he explains the seriousness of your case and makes it clear that there is little or no hope of recovery. Naturally you would ask how long was left to you, and the doctor would assure you that all possible help would be given. Whether the news came as a shock or whether it only confirmed what you already suspected, you would feel an inner turmoil and need time to settle down in quietness of spirit. Even those who are exceptionally strong in faith would surely have *some feeling of the awesomeness of meeting God*, however eagerly their spirits might be to see Him and adore Him. After all, there can be no worse valley to tread than the Valley of the Shadow of Death, but mercifully we do not tread it alone or go through it comfortless.

I well remember my first visit from my native Wales to the United States of America, with all the excitement of seeing that distant land and its many wonders for the first time. I had frequently flown to the Outer Hebrides of Scotland which were so dear to my heart, but to fly to America over that vast ocean was quite a new experience. The time came when all the preparations were made for the services and meetings, for packing clothes and changing currency, not forgetting passports and tickets, and at last we were on our way. However, as the plane drew within sight of the Great Lakes and we were informed of the weather conditions at our landing place in Detroit, I was suddenly filled with apprehension. Will they understand me? Will they like me? Will I like them? Thus my little mind filled itself with a host of queries about what awaited me. Then I arrived to be greeted with the smile and hug of kindly American friends and the welcome words, 'Hi, you guys!' But such a welcome is nothing to the arrival on the runway of glory and the ground conditions of heaven. God will be there and will meet me Himself. All our questions about what it will be like will be swept away in a flood of reassurances that all is well. Our God is the end of the journey.

Although it is difficult to express the matter in a logical sequence, there will be a *succession of realisations for us*.

One of the early thoughts will be concerning the One before whom I must shortly appear, and that is God Himself. From the Scriptures we will have learned something of the majesty of His person, and we may have been led to dwell upon those attributes that belong to Him as God and on those qualities of God with which we can relate to a certain degree by His grace. The more we do this, the more our hearts will be thrilled by what we learn. As we compare this world with the one to come and the God who is the centre of it all, we shall be overwhelmed by its sheer purity and we shall have a deep desire for such a place. We will have a longing to be with that glorious God who is our heavenly Father, for we are heirs of God and co-heirs with Christ (Romans 8:17).

The prospect of reaching such a glorious destination and the eternal security of being with God will be ours. We shall read our Scriptures and sing our psalms and hymns with a glowing melody of adoration and praise to God in our hearts. That God, who is love; that God, who is pure, will take us from a fallen world in all its sin and shame, safely home to Himself. It is because of the altogether lovely One, the Son of God, that we will be eternally grateful. The mind of the believer is overwhelmed with the reality that we shall be with Him and see Him as He is.

I have a yearning for that land,
Where the unnumbered throng

Extol the death on Calvary
In heaven's unending song.   *William Williams*

In preparing for heaven we will be aware of *a deep sense of our unworthiness*. This will have been present for a long time and it may flit through our minds again. I do not believe that there is anything wrong in such a thought, which is so well expressed in the hymn by Thomas Binney that we also considered in an earlier chapter:

Eternal Light! Eternal Light!
How pure the soul must be,
When, placed within Thy searching sight,
It shrinks not, but with calm delight,
Can live and look on Thee.

We cannot but ask who is worthy to enjoy such a sight, and yet to live? Momentarily a feeling of apprehension may fill our souls and our eyes flood with tears as we ask with the hymnist:

O how shall I, whose native sphere
Is dark, whose mind is dim,
Before the Ineffable appear,
And on my naked spirit bear
The uncreated beam?

It is hard to imagine how the eternal and holy God could possibly include me in His plans, yet He sent His only begotten Son to die for my sin. Love from so great and glorious a God to such a tiny, sinful mortal seems beyond comprehension, but it is true. Such is our assurance. It is not based on my worthiness but on the worthiness of my Lord and Saviour Jesus Christ. Oh how very privileged the Christian is!

Another likely reaction as we prepare to leave this world will be *a sense of nostalgia for what we know in life*, knowing that the Lord has done all things well for us. The beauty of mountains and valleys with villages nestling peacefully beside rivers may linger in our minds. But when we think spiritually we realise that there await us fairer sights and more beautiful views in glory. In any case our memory will retain clear impressions regarding all His creation. When we turn our thoughts to the lofty mountains of glory and the vast pastures of grace where there is the fount of living waters, we begin to realise something of the beauty of our heavenly home. We should prepare heart, mind and soul for life that is beyond description: 'Eye hath not seen, nor ear heard, neither hath entered into the heart (mind) of man, the things which God hath prepared for them that love Him' (1 Corinthians 2:9).

Some years ago an elderly lady from my congregation had to go into hospital for the first time in her life. I realised that she felt anxious and I prayed that God would be with her. When I visited her that evening she greeted me with a smile and could hardly wait to tell how she had been greatly helped by reading Psalm 46. 'Pastor,' she said, 'look at those words, "Be still".' Then she told me that she had been

practising this stillness of body and soul throughout
the day.

Once again on the following evening I found her
smiling and it was obvious she had more to tell me.
'Look again at those words, "Be still and know",' she
said, and then went on to relate how much she had
been guided and taught by the Lord in meditating on
the Psalm during the day.

The third evening she seemed to have a special
composure about her and she described how she had
been taken to the operating theatre in the morning.
When she recovered consciousness from the anaes-
thetic she saw bright lights and figures in white
speaking kindly to her. A sudden look of disappointment had showed in her face which caused the
doctors and nurses to be concerned about her, but she
had reassured them by explaining that she had thought
she had awakened in glory. As she recounted the
experience to me, she pointed my attention to the
remainder of the verse, 'Be still and know that I am
God.' That day the glory of God had filled her mind
and heart, and before it was over the disappointment
she had felt earlier turned to joy in His holy presence.
Let any nostalgia we have for this world be totally
eclipsed with the anticipation of being with God.

Another aspect of this matter which should occupy
our minds concerns *the promises of God and the
integrity of His person*. He is the God that cannot lie
(Titus 1:2) and in whom there is no variableness,

neither shadow of turning (James 1:17). He has promised an abundant entrance into the everlasting kingdom of our Lord and Saviour Jesus Christ (2 Peter 1:11). Flood your mind with promise after promise to His people regarding the reception that awaits them in heaven. We shall be met by God Himself and, although angels will bear us there, it is God who shall wipe all tears from our eyes.

Some time ago I was taking a funeral service during which I read the familiar passage of John 14: 'Let not your heart be troubled: ye believe in God, believe also in Me. In My Father's house are many mansions: if it were not so, I would have told you.' As I read that last phrase the reality of its meaning seemed to spring to life for me – the Lord is truthful and will not deceive us.

Afterwards as I shook hands at the door, most of the people appeared politely uninterested, but one man gripped my hand and said, 'God never lies.' Then as I went back inside to thank the old lady who had played the organ, she said, to my joy and amazement, 'Our God is truthful.' Each of us had grasped that wonderful truth that God is completely reliable and that He will never fail the frailest soul who trusts in Him. He will never forsake us but will be with us every step of the way. We are never out of His care and His promises will be kept. There will be no tears, hunger, thirst, pain or death where He is taking us.

Finally, in those last moments *let the peace of God be ours*. We know where we are going, we know whom we shall meet, we have glimpses in Scripture of what it will be like. Rest in His Word, lean on His person and go with Him with serenity of heart:

> My hand in Thine hold fast
> Till sorrow be o'erpast,
> And gentle death at last
> For heaven awake me.   *Robert Rowland Roberts*

There is a time to die. Millions have gone and will go this way. It is a well-trodden valley. For many it is a valley of despair and a dismal future. For others, they are guided to a place reserved for them in the heavenly Jerusalem. I remember being deeply impressed by a simple illustration in the book *Immortality* by Lorraine Boettner:

> I am standing upon the seashore. A ship at my side spreads her white sails to the morning breeze and starts for the blue ocean. She is an object of beauty and strength, and I stand and watch her until at length she hangs like a white cloud, just where the sea and the cloud meet each other. Then someone at my side says, 'There, she is gone.' Gone where? Gone from my sight, that is all. She is just as large in mast and hull and spar as she was when she left my side, and just as able to bear her load of living weights to its place of destination. Her diminished size is in me, not in her: and just at that moment when someone says at my side, 'There, she is gone,' on that distant shore there are other eyes watching for her coming and other voices ready to take up the glad shout, 'Here she comes!', and such is dying.